D1104371

A Shelf of Lincoln Books

A SHELF OF
LINCOLN BOOKS

A CRITICAL,

SELECTIVE BIBLIOGRAPHY

OF LINCOLNIANA

BY PAUL M. ANGLE

New Brunswick: Rutgers University Press

In Association with The Abraham Lincoln Association
of Springfield, Illinois

1946

COPYRIGHT 1946, BY

PAUL M. ANGLE

PRINTED IN THE UNITED STATES OF AMERICA

THE LAKESIDE PRESS, R. R. DONNELLEY & SONS COMPANY

CHICAGO, ILLINOIS

Author's Note

THIS book had its inception in an article entitled "Basic Lincolniana" which appeared in the *Bulletin* of the Abraham Lincoln Association for June and September, 1936. Some of the books covered in that article are not included here; a considerable number of new titles, most of which have appeared in recent years, have been added. The appraisals are, of course, much longer.

In my comments I have drawn freely upon reviews—my own, be it said—which have appeared in the *Bulletin* of the Abraham Lincoln Association and its successor, the *Abraham Lincoln Quarterly*, and in the book sections of the *New York Times*, the *New York Herald Tribune*, and the *Chicago Sun*. I hope that the reader will overlook the magisterial tone which I fear characterizes some of my comments. One may speak positively of demonstrable errors, but opinions are highly personal, and should, I think, be advanced with less assurance than I sometimes display.

One who writes even a small book incurs more obligations than he can repay by acknowledgments. I have one debt, however, which is too large to pass without mention. That is the debt which I owe to the Illinois State Historical Library. Not until I severed my connection with that institution did I realize the full extent of its superb resources.

PAUL M. ANGLE

Chicago
October, 1945

v

Contents

AUTHOR'S NOTE v

INTRODUCTION ix

WRITINGS AND SPEECHES 3

BIOGRAPHIES 17

MONOGRAPHS AND SPECIAL STUDIES . . . 65

BIBLIOGRAPHY 131

INDEX 137

Introduction

IN INTRODUCING this little book I could content myself with the summary statement of a few obvious truths. I could point to the great bulk of Lincoln literature,[1] and let readers themselves draw one sure inference—namely, that few students and fewer librarians have time to winnow the permanent from the inconsequential. I could show that many Lincoln books were little better than worthless when they were published, and that many others, good enough in their time, have lost much of the value they once possessed. I could demonstrate that many of those who have written about Lincoln had little equipment for the task except interest in the subject, and that in consequence Lincoln literature must be approached with more than usual caution. And thus I would have achieved the justification which every author who adds another Lincoln book considers obligatory.

These are, of course, valid reasons for a selective, critical bibliography, and most readers will find them sufficient. I hope, however, that there will be some who will be moved by a further reason that led me to undertake the writing of this book. I have found pleasure, interest, and I believe some enlightenment in knowing more than casually a great man and the period in which he lived, and I

[1]Jay Monaghan, in *Lincoln Bibliography, 1839-1939* (see p. 128) lists 3,958 books and pamphlets which are concerned in major part with Lincoln's life. No satisfactory bibliography of Lincoln articles in periodicals has been compiled, but the number of such articles certainly runs into four figures. And there are thousands of books which deal significantly, though not primarily, with Lincoln's career.

hope that this book will lead others to a similar reward.

Some years ago I met a man who was only a little short of one hundred years of age. He was the leading citizen of the town in which he lived, and still active in his law practice and several commercial enterprises. We talked about the great depression which had followed the crash of 1929. It had been bad, very bad, he admitted, but he had never lost heart. He remembered too many others—'57, '73, '93, and so on for almost a century. He had perspective. Few of us can count on achieving that quality by the accident of exceptional longevity, but vicarious experience is ours for the effort—and usually the pleasurable effort—of acquiring it.

For example. The country, you will hear it said, is going to hell at high speed. A short time ago I read a letter in which the writer proclaimed to his correspondent that he was "extremely mortified at our public proceedings; it appears to me that real Insanity has taken possession of mens minds." That was written in 1795,[2] and I suppose similar letters have been written, or similar sentiments expressed, ever since men began to live together. The tragedy is that so many people not only believe in incipient calamity, but act impulsively on the belief. Thus we have a Ku Klux Klan to combat the menace of the Roman Catholic Church and the foreign-born, a Father Coughlin to lead a crusade against Jews and communists. Given the perspective that comes from knowledge of the past—from knowledge, in this instance, of the rise and disintegration of the Know Nothing Party, of the sorry fate of the original Klan,

[2]The writer was John Langdon, of Portsmouth, N. H., one of the signers of the Constitution of the United States. The letter is in the collection of the Chicago Historical Society.

of the Red scare of the early 'twenties, of Jewish contributions to American life—and fewer men would lose their heads. That, at any rate, is my conviction.

This is not to say, of course, that the historical perspective does or should blind one to danger signals. But it should serve as a brake on impulse. He who possesses it is likely to ask whether what seems to be a sign of danger really is one, and insist on some evidence beyond mere mass conviction. Balance, rather than blindness, is its genuine and beneficial product.

Then there are the myriad lights which the past throws on the present. Who can begin to understand the attitude of Southern politicians towards the poll tax without knowing something of the Civil War and Reconstruction? Can anyone come to sound conclusions regarding the Negro problem unless he is familiar with the place the Negro has occupied in the American social fabric for at least the last century? How account for our curious and contradictory attitude towards Great Britain, for our puzzling mixture of friendliness and suspicion, without knowledge of many phases of American history—our national origins, our wars, our diplomacy, our German and Irish heritage? How can one understand our reluctance to adopt universal military service unless he knows our military history?

But these are utilitarian values. By their means history may lead to wisdom, although one would probably be hard put to show that historians, as a class, rank much above their fellowmen in their possession of that unusual virtue. There can be no doubt, however, about the fact that to a large number of its devotees history affords both interest and pleasure. The man who knows the past thoroughly can hardly help living a richer, more interesting life than the man to whom the past is only a dark void.

To illustrate the point, I submit one or two homely, personal illustrations. For a dozen years I lived in a house that faced what was once the fair grounds of Sangamon County, Illinois. The tract has long been devoted to ordinary urban uses, so that residences, small apartments, a public school, a Catholic academy and convent now stand there. But when I sat on my porch in the dark quiet of late summer evenings I could see more than a row of houses across the street. I could see thousands of delirious Republicans jamming those grounds one August day in 1860, hear the speakers shouting the praises of Old Abe Lincoln, and watch Lincoln himself barely escape from the cheering, crushing crowd when he made a personal appearance. I could look on as hundreds of Illinois farm boys stumbled through the manual of arms when Camp Yates was located on the old fair grounds in the spring of 1861. I could see, in my mind's eye, an undistinguished little man with reddish brown hair and a short beard assume command of the 21st Illinois Infantry, and I knew what none of those who were there at the time could have guessed—that in four years he was to receive Lee's surrender at Appomattox, and in four years more he was to take the presidential oath of office from the steps of the United States Capitol. Somehow, what I could bring from the past made living there richer by far than it would have been had I been able to see nothing but my neighbors' homes.

As I write these lines I look over Michigan Avenue to

Grant Park, and beyond it, Lake Michigan. From the avenue come the muffled roar of automobile engines and the swish of tires; beyond it a suburban train is passing; on the lake a regatta is in progress. But I can look down from my window and blot out one of the world's most famous streets and the park that lies beyond it. Where the traffic now moves in an endless line I can see the old lake shore, with the lake itself lying still as glass on a sultry August morning. I watch a straggling procession moving south along the beach—some Indians on horseback, a company of soldiers, women and children in wagons at the rear. And I know that only a mile or so farther on death will come to most of them in the Fort Dearborn Massacre. My view, absorbing as it is today, takes on another dimension from the past.

And one can do more, with a thorough knowledge of a segment of the past, than conjure up imaginary pictures. He can create a world into which he can slip at will, and for a man to have a retreat which no one else can penetrate is good for his soul. Suppose one's world is the England of Charles II. In his library, after a day in the hard and troublesome world of 1946, he can take the place, if he will, of Samuel Pepys. He can stand in awe while the Great Fire destroys hundreds of acres of his beloved London, catch a glimpse of the beauteous but wicked Nell Gwynne, and if he be so minded, indulge—with complete impunity—in peccadilloes which he neither could nor would permit himself in real life. He can live in another age—see its sights, hear its sounds, smell its smells, think its thoughts. He will come to know a great number of people whom it will be good to know—the clever, cynical, amusing king; his courtiers and mistresses; fellow-diarists like John Evelyn; John Dryden, poet and dramatist; the Earl of Clarendon, statesman and historian; and a host of actors and actresses, musicians, servant girls, and shady characters who are likely to be even more interesting than the great men and women of the time.

From such an experience, repeated effortlessly, he cannot fail to profit. His excursions into other times will often be almost as rejuvenating as his actual vacation trips. He will have the great satisfaction that comes from knowing anything thoroughly. He will be able to correct, from his own sure knowledge, much misinformation that he will encounter, and for the remainder of his life he will be healthily skeptical of the printed page. He will find himself endowed with new understanding, greater tolerance, and more humility.

Any period in history offers these rewards. One can make a case for the Age of Pericles or the Rome of Augustus, for Shakespeare's England or Samuel Johnson's, for the France of Louis XIV or the French Revolution, for the Italian Renaissance, for the Ireland of George Moore, Synge, and Yeats, to name only a few. Not many periods, however, can approach in their potentialities the United States in the time of Abraham Lincoln.

The advantages of that period are many. First among them, perhaps, is the geographical scope of Lincoln's life. An average American interested in Anthony Trollope will be fortunate to visit "Barsetshire" once in his lifetime. That same American, interested in Lincoln, will have many opportunities for experiencing that feeling of intimacy that comes from standing in places where a man of the past actually lived. Kentucky, Indiana, Illinois, and Washington by no means exhaust the places associated with Lincoln's life. Iowa, Kansas, Missouri, Wisconsin, Michigan, and Ohio treasure the memory of his visits; Massachusetts, Pennsylvania, New Jersey, and Virginia are proud of having harbored his ancestors. Moreover, if one extends his interest beyond Lincoln biography to the Civil War, there is hardly a locality in the eastern half of the country without its associations.

In the second place, the extensive literature that makes a book of this kind desirable is itself a good reason for choosing Lincoln as a subject. The materials for knowing the man and his time are readily available. Many of the books described in the following pages are on the shelves of every good-sized public library, and with the exception of a dozen titles, all can be purchased from the publishers or from antiquarian booksellers for modest sums. No real enthusiast, however, will confine himself to this list. Before long he will discover that *The Diary of Orville Hickman Browning*, not included here, throws lights of rare quality on Lincoln's life. If he becomes interested in Browning, the chances are that he will find his way sooner or later to Usher F. Linder's inimitable *Reminiscences of the Early Bench and Bar of Illinois*. Linder may lead to Ford's *History of Illinois*, and that, perhaps, to a neglected American classic, the *Memoirs of Gustave Koerner*. The direction of one's tangential interests makes little difference. Lincoln's associates, his background, the Civil War—on these and all related subjects the books exist, and anyone can find them easily.

Lincoln's associates, by the way, offer a particularly fascinating field for study. Most Americans have a hazy recollection from school history days of Seward, Stanton, Cameron, Welles, Chase, and a few of the best known military leaders. If they remember anything, they remember stereotypes—the dynamic Stanton, who organized the armies and people of the North for victory; the cool, capable, incorruptible Chase, who financed the war; the vacillating McClellan who almost lost it; and so forth. But when they get beneath the surface of history the stereotypes vanish and they find themselves in the midst of hot argument. Was Stanton really capable, or was he only a cowardly tyrant who made himself a reputation by bluster and rudeness? Or worse? Chase incorruptible? In the financial sense, yes, but what did his ambition do to his moral fibre? McClellan vacillating? As soon as one passes his novitiate in Civil War history he encounters a school of students who hold that McClellan was the North's greatest commander! Before long, one comes to know these men almost as friends and enemies.

The Lincoln period, moreover, has the advantage of not being so remote in time that one has to strain to find connections with the present. One takes the Alton Railroad from Chicago to Springfield, and realizes that that road, like most of the other main lines that now serve the Middle West, was begun in the last decade of Lincoln's career at the Illinois bar. If he chooses the Illinois Central for the same trip, he will be traveling on a road which for several years retained Lincoln as one of its attorneys. The steel plow and the reaper, still basic in agriculture, came into existence in his maturity. The factory system had just begun to displace handcraftsmen, at least in the Old Northwest, when he assumed the presidency. And centralization in government, which remains one of our most crucial problems, is generically connected with his administration.

But the best of all reasons for studying Lincoln's life is the fact that he was a truly great man. He not only influenced the course of history; he also exemplified those virtues to which civilized man has given his highest allegiance—steadfastness, faith in righteousness, humility, and the forgiving spirit. At the same time his humor, his earthiness, his utter lack of pretension made him one with common humanity. To spend time—much time—in such a man's company can be one of life's privileges.

A Shelf of Lincoln Books

PART ONE

Writings and Speeches

THE one indispensable component of a shelf of Lincoln books, no matter how small, is Lincoln's own writings and speeches. Their importance as historical material is obvious. So is their current usefulness, for no great American is quoted—and misquoted—more often than Lincoln. Their value to the general reader, though often overlooked, is hardly less great. Far more than most men, Lincoln "expressed himself" in what he said and wrote. For a reader to supplement Allen Johnson's *Stephen A. Douglas* by going through all Douglas's writings would be a waste of time, but anyone who does not go on from the best biographies of Lincoln to what he himself wrote and said stops short of full understanding.

NICOLAY AND HAY.
COMPLETE WORKS OF ABRAHAM LINCOLN. 1894.

Not until twenty-nine years after Lincoln's death was an inclusive collection of his writings available. Then the impulse came from Robert T. Lincoln, who wrote on May 30, 1893, to John G. Nicolay:

My dear Nicolay: As you and Colonel Hay have now brought your great work to a most successful conclusion by the publication of your life of my father, I hope and request that you and he will supplement it by collecting, editing, and publishing the speeches, letters, state papers, and miscellaneous writings of my father. You and Colonel Hay have my consent and authority to obtain for yourselves such protection by copyright, or otherwise, in respect to the whole or any part of such a collection, as I might for any reason be entitled to have.[1]

In the following year appeared the *Complete Works of Abraham Lincoln*, edited by John G. Nicolay and John Hay. In two thick volumes 1736 letters, speeches, miscellaneous writings, and the full text of the Lincoln-Douglas debates were presented to the public.

For its time it was an admirable production, but the present-day student finds it inadequate. Hundreds, perhaps thousands, of Lincoln's writings have come to light since it was published; and modern historical scholarship is more exacting than it was fifty years ago.

Take, for example, the matter of textual accuracy. Here is a letter from Lincoln to Edward Lusk, October 30, 1858, as Nicolay and Hay rendered it:

Dear Sir: I understand the story is still being told and insisted upon that I have been a Know-nothing. I repeat what I stated in a public speech at Meredosia, that I am not, nor ever have been, connected with the party called the Know-nothing party, or party calling themselves the American party. Certainly no man of truth, and I believe no man of good character for truth, can be found to say on his own knowledge that I was ever connected with that party.

Here is the same letter as it would be reproduced today by a careful editor:

Dear Sir: I understand the story is still being told, and insisted upon, that I have been a Know Nothing— I repeat, what I stated in a public speech at Meredosia, that I am not, nor ever have been, connected with the party called the Know Nothing party, or party calling themselves the American party— *Certainly* no man of truth, and I *believe*, no man

[1]Preface, *Complete Works of Abraham Lincoln.*

[of] good character for truth can be found to say on his own knowledge that I ever was connected with that party—[2]

In this example the editors' changes, which were obviously inspired by regard for orthodoxy and uniformity, had little if any effect upon the meaning of the original. The case is somewhat different, however, with a document like the House Divided speech of June 16, 1858. There editorial tidying stripped a forceful utterance of much of its original emphasis. The first sentences of that speech, as they appear in the *Complete Works*, follow:

> If we could first know where we are, and whither we are tending, we could better judge what to do, and how to do it. We are now far into the fifth year since a policy was initiated with the avowed object and confident promise of putting an end to slavery agitation. Under the operation of that policy, that agitation has not only not ceased, but has constantly augmented. In my opinion, it will not cease until a crisis shall have been reached and passed.

Today a competent editor would print these sentences as they are to be found in the *Illinois State Journal* of June 18, 1858, which published the speech from Lincoln's manuscript and under his supervision:

> If we could first know *where* we are, and *whither* we are tending, we could then better judge *what* to do, and *how* to do it.
>
> We are now far into the *fifth* year, since a policy was initiated, with the *avowed* object, and *confident* promise, of putting an end to slavery agitation.
>
> Under the operation of that policy, that agitation has not only, *not ceased*, but has *constantly augmented*.
>
> In *my* opinion, it *will* not cease, until a *crisis* shall have been reached, and passed.

In fairness, it should be said that there is no evidence that Nicolay and Hay ever purposely distorted meaning. Such changes as they made were dictated by what would now be

[2]Transcribed from the original in the Illinois State Historical Library.

considered undue regard for form. The blue pencil was not part of their editorial equipment.

The *Complete Works* has one other deficiency. That is the paucity of editorial explanation. The First Inaugural Address, for example, is presented without any account of the evolution of the text, although the editors had devoted an entire chapter—Chapter XXI in Volume III—to the subject in *Abraham Lincoln: A History*. No distinction is made between the various texts of the Gettysburg Address. As a rule, neither recipients of letters nor persons mentioned in them are identified; most allusions, no matter how obscure, are passed by without notice. The location of originals, or the location of other sources from which texts were taken, is given only in a minute number of instances. In fact, there are fewer than two dozen footnotes or editorial interpolations in nearly 1400 pages of text.

But lapses in textual accuracy and deficiencies in editorial explanation are not likely to be of much consequence except to research workers. The two-volume *Complete Works* contains all Lincoln's important speeches and state papers, and a majority of his important letters. The general reader, the small library, and the collector whose ambitions do not go beyond a shelf of modest size, will find that it satisfies nearly all needs.

NICOLAY AND HAY.
    COMPLETE WORKS OF ABRAHAM LINCOLN. 1905.

The large library, the collector intent upon assembling a big collection, and the research worker cannot be satisfied with anything less than the most inclusive collection of Lincoln's writings. That is the *Complete Works of Abraham Lincoln,* published in twelve volumes by the Francis D. Tandy Co., New York, 1905. The book bears the names of Nicolay and Hay as editors, but the actual editor appears to have been Francis D. Tandy.

In introducing the Tandy Edition attention was called to the fact that a decade had passed since the two-volume *Complete Works* had appeared. "During that period," the editor continued, "the assiduity of a multitude of Lincoln collectors has brought to light a large amount of manuscript material which inevitably escaped even such conscientious workers as Nicolay and Hay. . . . The aim has been to collect this material, add it to the work of the two great biographers, and so make a complete and definitive edition."

In comparing this book with its predecessor one should beware of jumping to conclusions based upon comparative size. The text is printed in large type heavily leaded; margins are wide; and the paper has what the printer calls "bulk." The earlier work, on the other hand, is compactly printed on paper of relatively low bulk. The Tandy Edition, consequently, is by no means six times the size of the two-volume collection.

Actually, the Tandy Edition added 518 separate items to the 1736 in the first Nicolay and Hay compilation. The latter, therefore, contains almost eighty per cent of the writings and speeches printed in the "complete and definitive edition." If a qualitative standard is applied, the difference between the two collections becomes even smaller.

Every important speech, every important state paper, is to be found in the earlier collection. (Perhaps an exception should be made in the case of Lincoln's speech before the Illinois legislature, January 11, 1837, which is to be found only in the Tandy Edition.) The 518 additional items are almost entirely letters. Without them, our knowledge of Lincoln's life and character would be less full than it is. Nevertheless, the level of significance of the added items is appreciably lower than the level of the original 1736.

Only by virtue of its greater scope is the Tandy Edition markedly superior to the two-volume *Complete Works*. Its texts show no advance in accuracy. In fact, all items in the original edition were reprinted without change; all new items were recast with the same over-solicitude (by modern standards) for orthodoxy in spelling, punctuation, and form. Editorial notes are more numerous, but still far below a desirable number. More sources of texts are located, but in the great majority of instances they remain unrevealed.

The Tandy Edition, moreover, contains one fabrication, and one speech and one saying of doubtful authenticity, all of which are to be found in the added material. The fabrication is the item headed, "Extracts of a Letter to George E. Pickett," February 22, 1842 (Vol. I, 191–92), which, though of little consequence of itself, has attracted much attention because of Pickett's later prominence as a Confederate general. The doubtful speech, dated March, 1832, is cautiously labelled, "Reputed First Political Speech" (Vol. XI, 97–98). Its source, which was not indicated by the editor, was a man's recollection half a century after its reputed delivery. The saying, "You can fool all the people some of the time and some of the people all of the time, but you cannot fool all the people all the time," is offered with editorial reservations (Vol. III, 349n), but its genuineness is open to even stronger question than the editor implies.

The Tandy Edition also contains fourteen misdated letters and speeches. (Several of these were incorrectly dated in the two-volume *Complete Works*, and were reprinted without change.) All are listed below:[3]

Address Before the Young Men's Lyceum of Springfield, I, 35–50
    Misdated January 27, 1837
    Correct date: January 27, 1838

Letter to John J. Hardin, I, 271–74
    Misdated January 19, 1845
    Correct date: January 19, 1846

Bill to Abolish Slavery in the District of Columbia, II, 96–100
    Misdated January 16, 1849
    Correct date: January 10, 1849

Letter to John D. Johnston, II, 144–46
    Misdated January [2?], 1851
    Correct date: Washington, December 24, 1848

Letter to Charles Hoyt, II, 146–47
    Misdated January 11, 1851
    Correct date: Springfield, January 16, 1856

Letter to A. B. Morean, XI, 100
    Misdated March 23, 1855, and misspelled "Moreau"
    Correct date: September 7, 1854

Fragment of Speech at Galena, II, 292–95
    Misdated August [1?], 1856
    Correct date: July 23, 1856

Speech at Clinton, Illinois, III, 349–56
    Misdated September 8, 1858
    Correct date: September 2, 1858

[3]For the evidence establishing correct dates, see *Bulletin* of the Abraham Lincoln Association, No. 24, September, 1931, 7-9.

Fragment of Speech at Paris, Illinois, XI, 105–06
   Misdated September 8, 1858
   Correct date: September 7, 1858

Fragment of Speech at Edwardsville, Illinois, XI, 106–11
   Misdated September 13, 1858
   Correct date: September 11, 1858

Letter to Alexander Sympson, V, 89
   Misdated Blandinsville, October 26, 1858
   Correct date: Blandinsville, October 24, 1858

Remarks at Springfield, VI, 49–50
   Misdated August 14, 1860
   Correct date: August 8, 1860

Letter to Benjamin F. Butler, VIII. 167–68
   Misdated January 2, 1863
   Correct date: Washington, January 2, 1864

Reply to a Committee of Congress, XI, 10
   Misdated February 9, 1865
   Correct date: February 26, 1861

In promoting the Tandy Edition, the publisher emphasized not only the added material, but also a number of "special features"—special introductions to each volume, an anthology of Lincoln's sayings, a chronological index, and the "Lincoln Bibliography" of Daniel Fish, which takes up almost half of Volume XI. This bibliography, valuable in its day, has now been superseded by the *Lincoln Bibliography* of Jay Monaghan;[4] the special introductions and chronological index were never much more than selling points. The anthology, though far from exhaustive, is still useful.

Despite its imperfections, the Tandy Edition is clearly superior to a rival work published during the same year— *Writings of Abraham Lincoln*, edited by Arthur Brooks Lap-

[4]See p. 128.

sley (New York, Putnam, 1905; 8 volumes). The Tandy Edition is larger by a third than the Lapsley book; while the Lapsley book contains nothing of importance not to be found in the Tandy Edition except the text of Lincoln's "Lost Speech" of May 29, 1856. And that is spurious.[5]

GILBERT A. TRACY.
UNCOLLECTED LETTERS OF ABRAHAM LINCOLN. 1917.

"Few, if any, items of importance can any longer be hidden," wrote the publisher of the *Complete Works of Abraham Lincoln* in 1905.[6] Yet within a quarter of a century three supplementary volumes of Lincoln letters, papers, and speeches were to be published, and today several hundred more are known to be outside of any compilation.

The first of these additional volumes to appear was *Uncollected Letters of Abraham Lincoln*, brought together by Gilbert A. Tracy. Here are 359 letters, telegrams, notes, and endorsements not to be found in the *Complete Works of Abraham Lincoln*. There are no speeches. Many of the letters are important, but the qualitative average of the collection is lower than that of the two inclusive compilations which preceded it. A good half of the letters, and nearly all the important ones, represent the pre-presidential period of Lincoln's life.

In editorial proficiency, the Tracy volume marks a distinct advance. Tracy transcribed his texts with a fair degree of accuracy, although by no means perfectly; in most cases

[5] See p. 80.
[6] Quoted from the Prospectus.

he indicated either the ownership of the original letter or the printed source from which he took a copy; and he supplied many explanatory footnotes. Unfortunately, he included four letters which are clearly spurious. These are addressed and dated as follows:

To Peter Hitchcock, Cincinnati, December 24, 1849. ("Spurious" is hardly the right word to apply to this letter. The evidence indicates that it is a genuine letter but that the author was Timothy D. Lincoln, a well known admiralty lawyer of Cincinnati, rather than Abraham Lincoln.)

To James Lemen, Springfield, March 2, 1857.

To John J. Crittenden, Springfield, December 22, 1859.

To Alexander H. Stephens, Springfield, January 19, 1860.[7]

In addition, the Tracy volume contains one incorrectly dated letter—that to Gustave Koerner on p. 77. As printed, the date is given as July 10, 1857. The original letter, in the Henry E. Huntington Library, is clearly dated July 19, 1857.

PAUL M. ANGLE.
NEW LETTERS AND PAPERS OF LINCOLN. 1930.

In *New Letters and Papers of Lincoln* the compiler assembled 430 letters, speeches, legal opinions, and miscellaneous writings not to be found in either the *Complete Works of Abraham Lincoln* or Tracy's *Uncollected Letters*. Although many items of real significance are presented—Lincoln's

[7]The case against these letters is presented in the *Bulletin* of the Abraham Lincoln Association, No. 21, December, 1930.

Eulogy on Zachary Taylor, for example, and the speech before the Springfield Scott Club—the volume falls below the Tracy collection in interest and importance. This may be partly accounted for by the fact that each successive supplementary volume pays a heavier tax under the law of diminishing returns, and partly by the editor's decision to defer to the ever-growing interest in Lincoln's life and include notes and endorsements which earlier compilers would have rejected as inconsequential.

Editorially, *New Letters and Papers of Lincoln* meets modern standards of scholarship. In every instance, the location of the original letter or primary printed source is indicated. Texts are accurately transcribed. Annotation at least approaches adequacy. Unfortunately, the compiler attempted to ensnare a sizable number of non-specialist readers by shaping his editorial contributions into short prefaces and tail-pieces for each letter or speech. The general reader was not beguiled, and the sole result was a format less usable by the specialist than would have been the case had the editor's offerings taken the orthodox form of footnotes.

EMANUEL HERTZ.
ABRAHAM LINCOLN: A NEW PORTRAIT.
1931.

On the heels of *New Letters and Papers of Lincoln* came *Abraham Lincoln: A New Portrait*, by Emanuel Hertz. The first volume of this work consists of speeches which Hertz made on various phases of Lincoln's life; the second volume is made up of Lincoln's own writings. "I have taken all," Hertz explained, "be they long or short, be they formal or intimate, whatever he [Lincoln] wrote or spoke I have assembled—all to be published at some future day—always provided that the item has not appeared in its complete or exact form in the Tandy-Gettysburg edition of Lincoln's works, nor in the Putnam-Lapsley edition, nor in the Tracey [*sic*] collection nor in the pioneer work of Ida M. Tarbell and contained in the last editions of her 'Life of Lincoln.'" He added that he had included "some items" which appeared in Angle's *New Letters and Papers of Lincoln*.

The Hertz collection does contain many interesting and valuable items not to be found elsewhere, but it hardly lives up to the compiler's contention that it was a supplement to earlier volumes. A tabulation shows that it includes sixty-six items which are to be found in the Tandy Edition, thirty-three which appear in Tracy, and 161 which were published in Angle—nearly two-fifths of the book.

Moreover, the editor performed his work with complete disregard for any standard of scholarship. He included, without explanation of any kind, some thirty conversations of doubtful genuineness; he lifted line after line verbatim from Angle's notes; he printed many excerpts without even approximate dates and without the names of recipients; he misdated many letters; and he was duped by more forgeries and fabrications than appear in all other compilations of Lincoln's writings put together. These last are listed below:

Speech, May 6, 1842, at Cincinnati, p. 531.
Letter to Macedonio Melloni,[8] pp. 623–25.

[8]For a conclusive demonstration of the spurious character of this letter, which "comes to light" at fairly frequent intervals, see Raymond G. Rocca, "Fascist Propaganda and a Lincoln Forgery," *Abraham Lincoln Quarterly*, December, 1943, 370–77.

Speech at Urbana, October 4, 1854,[9] pp. 627–55.

Promissory Note to L. S. Benedict, p. 791.

Letter to the Secretaries of the St. Marie Brass Band and St. Cecilia Society, p. 791.

Memorandum on Corporations and Corruption, p. 954.

Letter to E. D. Taylor, p. 957.

The defects of the second volume of *Abraham Lincoln: A New Portrait* are so many and so serious that one should not rely on it for any text that can be found elsewhere, nor should one use a text that cannot be found elsewhere without first testing it, when possible, by independent evidence.

PHILIP VAN DOREN STERN.

THE LIFE AND WRITINGS OF ABRAHAM LINCOLN. 1940.

Of the books so far described in this section, all are of primary utility to the more-than-casual student. The general reader—the person who reads what Lincoln wrote principally to find out what kind of man he was—will probably consider them all, with the possible exception of the two-volume Nicolay and Hay collection, too large or too specialized for his purpose. But for him *The Life and Writings of Abraham Lincoln*[10] should serve most purposes.

This collection comprises 274 items—the largest grouping of its kind to be found in a single volume. The editor has omitted parts of many letters and speeches, but even so, five long speeches are printed in their entirety—those at Peoria (October 16, 1854), Kalamazoo (August 27, 1856),

---

[9]For this speech see p. 80.

[10]Published originally by Random House, 1940. In 1942 it was reprinted, after a number of corrections had been made, as a Modern Library Giant. The latter edition is the more desirable.

the House Divided, Cooper Union, and First Inaugural addresses. The selection is admirable, the excerpting skilfully done. Each item, moreover, is introduced by a prefatory statement that places it in its contemporary setting.

In addition to Lincoln's writings, the editor has supplied a long biographical sketch that is a small book in itself. There is also a chronology of Lincoln's life. Only the index leaves anything to be desired.

Roy P. Basler.
   ABRAHAM LINCOLN: HIS SPEECHES AND WRITINGS. 1946.

For the scholar, Basler's selection is clearly superior to Stern's, and many general readers will find it equally satisfactory. The collection, chosen for literary significance, historical importance, and human interest, comprises 228 items to Stern's 274, but every letter or speech is complete. Moreover, Basler's is the only general collection of Lincoln's writings in which a successful effort to achieve textual accuracy has been made. In more than three-fourths of his selections the editor has taken his text from the original document or a photostatic copy of it; for the remainder he has relied upon the best authenticated printed version. Like Stern, he introduces each selection by a prefatory statement.

In an Introduction of considerable length Basler discusses the devices by which Lincoln, often unconsciously, gave vent to his "love of words and symbols and his eternal craving to entertain people and to create beauty." His analysis, though occasionally somewhat technical, is both keen and sound.

PART TWO

Biographies

WILLIAM DEAN HOWELLS.

LIFE OF ABRAHAM LINCOLN. 1860 and 1938.

UNLESS one wants to know what the people of Lincoln's own time knew about him, only one of the books written before his death is worth reading today. And that one derives its importance not from intrinsic merit, but because a fortunate chance gave one copy, reprinted in 1938, autobiographical status.

When Lincoln was nominated for the presidency in 1860 the publishing firm of Follett, Foster, and Company of Columbus, Ohio was one of several which rushed to get a biography of the nominee into print. To produce it they chose a young editorial writer on the *Ohio State Journal*—William Dean Howells. Howells sent a law student named James Quay Howard to Springfield to interview Lincoln and his old friends, and to gather material from other sources. From Howard's memoranda Howells wrote the book which, with the addition of several of Lincoln's speeches and a short sketch of Hannibal Hamlin, appeared on June 25, 1860, as *Lives and Speeches of Abraham Lincoln and Hannibal Hamlin*.[1]

[1]For a full bibliographical description of this book and a discussion of its place among campaign biographies, see Ernest J. Wessen, "Campaign Lives of Abraham Lincoln, 1860," in *Papers in Illinois History, 1937* (Springfield, Illinois State Historical Society, 1938). A later edition includes a much longer section, "Life and Speeches of Hannibal Hamlin," by John L. Hayes.

Sometime during the summer of 1860 Samuel C. Parks, an old friend and fellow lawyer of Lincoln, asked the nominee to correct his copy of the Howells book. Lincoln complied, and it is obvious from the character of his notations that he took the task seriously. Some of his corrections pertain to minor matters, some to points of consequence. By inference, the statements that he allowed to stand may be considered authoritative.

In 1938 the Abraham Lincoln Association obtained permission to publish a facsimile reprint of the Parks copy of the Howells *Life*.[2] Since nearly all Lincoln's corrections fall in the biographical section, only that part was reprinted. The book, like all other campaign lives, is a mere sketch, running only to 7,500 words. Approximately a third of the text is devoted to Lincoln's life at New Salem, a phase of his subject's career which seems to have caught Howells' fancy, and which he treated with color and zest. Since this period of Lincoln's life has been described principally from reminiscences, which are rarely very trustworthy, the fullness of Howells' treatment is particularly fortunate.

The reprint has a preface in which the writing of the book is described and its importance appraised. There also a number of errors which Lincoln failed to correct are noted and their significance estimated.

JOSIAH G. HOLLAND.
    THE LIFE OF ABRAHAM LINCOLN. 1866.

The tragic and dramatic death of Lincoln gave rise to a flood of writings about him. By far the best of these was the

[2]The book is now in the collection of the Illinois State Historical Library.

biography written by J. G. Holland, well known then as a novelist and as one of the editors of the *Springfield Republican*.

A full-length biography, Holland's book opens with a brief but untrustworthy account of Lincoln's boyhood in Kentucky and Indiana. The author's treatment of his subject's early years in Illinois is much more detailed and much sounder. Holland interviewed Herndon and other friends and associates of Lincoln, and from them obtained not a few anecdotes which still repay the attention of a reader. After Lincoln emerged as an important figure—about 1854 —the narrative is concerned principally with his record, and little attention is paid to motivation. (Holland, for example, gives no account of Lincoln's attitude towards secession as the movement became an increasing menace, nor does he mention the considerations that influenced Lincoln's choice of his cabinet.) Nevertheless, the account of Lincoln's presidency is a good review of salient features— of military operations, foreign affairs, emancipation, the election of 1864, the assassination and funeral. Here again anecdotes and reminiscences enliven the text.

Holland's *Life* reflected the conception of Lincoln that prevailed immediately after his death; it also tended to mold that conception into a pattern that was to persist unchanged for many years. Lincoln's poverty-stricken childhood, his passion for learning, the spiritual character of his mother, his honesty, his simplicity, his deep sense of justice —these are favorite themes. Yet the book is more than extended adulation. Holland did not shrink from Lincoln's earthiness, although he felt called upon to excuse it. Somehow, he caught a perception of what most modern students consider Lincoln's essential characteristics as a lawyer—his habit of searching reflection, and his reliance upon general principles rather than great learning in case law. Even more remarkably, he did not present Lincoln as an anti-slavery crusader, nor as a reformer in any other sphere.

In accordance with the proprieties of his time, Holland almost ignored the intimate side of Lincoln's life. The romance with Ann Rutledge, which Herndon had not yet made public, is of course omitted. No mention is made of Mary Owens. Lincoln's marriage is covered in one paragraph, without allusion to the broken engagement. And Mrs. Lincoln's eccentricities are passed over entirely.

One feature of Holland's biography gave rise to long and bitter controversy. That was his emphasis, in the concluding pages, upon Lincoln's Christianity. A single sentence sums up his point of view: "Moderate, frank, truthful, gentle, forgiving, loving, just, Mr. Lincoln will always be remembered as eminently a Christian President; and the almost immeasurably great results which he had the privilege of achieving, were due to the fact that he was a Christian President." This kind of thing was a red flag to William H. Herndon, who drew heavily upon a vituperative vocabulary in combatting it. Since his day the controversy has declined in acrimony, but the nature and depth of Lincoln's religion are still an open question.

Ward Hill Lamon.
  THE LIFE OF ABRAHAM LINCOLN. 1872.

Ward Hill Lamon was the first Lincoln biographer to challenge the filio-pietistic school.

Lamon had been one of Lincoln's few close friends. Their intimacy went back to the early 'fifties when Lamon, a young lawyer of Danville, Illinois, became the older man's partner in the trial of cases in the eastern part of the eighth circuit. Lincoln's rising political fortunes had no effect upon their relations. On his journey to Washington for the inauguration he took Lamon along as friend and personal bodyguard, and as soon as he became President he appointed him Marshal of the District of Columbia. Lamon's impulsiveness and high-handed behavior caused many complaints, but Lincoln, aware of his utter loyalty, never wavered in his support and affection.

This close friendship was a matter of common knowledge. Readers, therefore, were totally unprepared for what they found in Lamon's biography. The first three sentences set the tone:

"Abraham Lincoln was born on the twelfth day of February, 1809. His father's name was Thomas Lincoln, and his mother's maiden name was Nancy Hanks. *At the time of his birth, they are supposed to have been married about three years*."[3]

There was more, much more, to follow. Thomas Lincoln was "idle, thriftless, poor, a hunter, and a rover." Lincoln's parents were married only by "mutual acknowledgment and cohabitation"; their home on Nolin Creek was a "miserable cabin." Lincoln himself was by no means sacrosanct. "His engagement to Miss Todd was one of the great misfortunes of his life and of hers." "But his humor was not of a delicate quality; it was chiefly exercised in hearing and telling stories of the grosser sort." "On the whole, he was an

[3]My italics.

honest, although a shrewd, and by no means an unselfish politician." And of course he was an infidel.

The disparity between this approach and Lamon's proved loyalty to Lincoln quickly gave rise to the charge that he was not the real author. Rumor named Chauncey F. Black, the son of Buchanan's Attorney General. Forty years were to pass, however, before the rumor was clearly substantiated, and not until 1938 was the full story published.[4]

Briefly, these are the facts. Lamon had a fund of personal information about Lincoln, but was incapable of writing a connected narrative; Black had inside knowledge of national politics and literary skill. The two men joined forces. Lamon agreed to make available the copies of the biographical data he had purchased from Herndon, Black was to do the actual writing—though Lamon's name was to appear as sole author—and the profits were to be divided. Black worked rapidly and completed the manuscript of the first volume, but while it was in proofs the collaborators fell out over the question of revisions. In the end, some parts of the manuscript were toned down, a final chapter was suppressed, and a projected second volume was never even commenced.[5]

As a publishing venture, the book was a failure. Most reviewers were severely critical, and only 1900 copies were disposed of.

Considered on its merits, there is much to be said for the Lamon biography. Admittedly, Black occasionally went too

[4]Albert V. House, Jr., "The Trials of a Ghost-Writer of Lincoln Biography," *Journal* of the Illinois State Historical Society, September, 1938.
[5]*Ibid.*, 295.

far in the direction of detraction, and sometimes his partizanship is obvious, but on the whole he made skilful use of his material. His account of Lincoln's Indiana boyhood, young manhood, and years in the Illinois legislature is vivid and detailed—a better exploitation, in fact, of Herndon's sources than Herndon and Weik achieved. He overemphasized the part that mere expediency played in Lincoln's political advancement, but later research has shown that his story of the deals that were made at the Chicago convention was more than scandalous gossip. In a word his realism, though sometimes exaggerated, had a solid basis.

Moreover, the emphasis on intimate phases of Lincoln's life is still welcome to a reading public whose interest extends to the smallest personal detail. In sharp contrast to Holland, the Lamon biography contains full accounts of Lincoln's relations with Ann Rutledge and Mary Owens, and of his troubled courtship of Mary Todd, including the closely related near-duel with Shields. Also in sharp contrast is the detailed exposition of Lincoln's infidelity—inflammable fuel in a controversy then white hot.

Twenty-three years after the publication of Lamon's *Life* another book with his name on the title page made its appearance. That was the *Recollections of Abraham Lincoln, 1847–1865, by Ward Hill Lamon.* Again there was an intermediary—Lamon having been dead two years—but this time it was his daughter. Of the *Recollections* she wrote in her preface: "Some of it has been taken from serious manuscript which my father intended for a work of history, some from articles written in a lighter vein; much has been gleaned from copies of letters which he wrote to friends, but most

has been gathered from notes jotted down on a multitude
of scraps scattered through a mass of miscellaneous material." Albert V. House has further clarified the source of
this volume. "In the Lamon collection of 2,400 items in the
Henry E. Huntington Library, is a typed manuscript con-
taining a disconnected series of recollections, anecdotes,
etc., with autographed corrections by Lamon. This was
used by Dorothy Lamon Teillard as the basis for her volume of her father's *Recollections of Lincoln.*"[6]

The *Recollections*, much more personal and anecdotal than
the *Life*, is a book of considerable interest. A second edition,
enlarged by the addition of a memoir of Lamon, other reminiscences, and correspondence received by Lamon, was
published in 1911.

Isaac N. Arnold.
THE LIFE OF ABRAHAM LINCOLN. 1885.

Isaac N. Arnold knew Lincoln for a quarter of a century.
After 1840 the two men came in frequent contact in the
courts of the state; later they were associated in Republican
politics. In 1860, moreover, Arnold was elected to Congress
from the Chicago district, and two years afterward he was
re-elected. Throughout Lincoln's administration he was
one of the President's staunchest supporters. He was also
one of his closest personal friends.

Before Lincoln's death Arnold commenced the book that
was published in 1866 under the title, *History of Abraham
Lincoln and the Overthrow of Slavery*. As the title implies, it was
too heavily cumbered with history to be a satisfactory biog-

[6]*Journal* of the Illinois State Historical Society, September, 1938, 295n.

raphy. Arnold himself perceived that fact and eventually undertook a book in which Lincoln would be the center of interest. He finished it in the year of his death, and it was published posthumously.

Like Holland, Arnold subscribed to the conventions of his day. His *Life*, therefore, is marked by decorum. He wrote sketchily and discreetly of his subject's personal life, and he never hinted at any lapses or indiscretions. He did, however, devote considerable space to Lincoln's professional career, and since that was a subject of which he had first-hand knowledge, his account is valuable. In line with the prevailing interest of readers of the time, he devoted two-thirds of his space to Lincoln's administration.

But while Arnold rarely wrote intimately of Lincoln, he did not feel obliged to submerge himself completely in the impersonal biographer. His own recollections are often set down, especially in the footnotes. Because he knew the men of whom he wrote, his characterizations of members of Congress and officials of the government are valuable. He wrote at length of emancipation and the attitude of Congress towards it—a subject on which he was well qualified. The book concludes with a fine character sketch and an estimate of Lincoln's place in history.

Arnold was a man of scholarly tastes and instincts, and one who put a high premium on historical accuracy. Nevertheless, his work is not without factual faults. His Nancy Hanks, to cite one example, is a fluent reader, although it appears to be certain that the real Nancy Hanks could neither read nor write. An error of that kind can be explained on the assumption that the documents which would have revealed the facts were inaccessible to the biographer, but Arnold should have known better than to assert, as he did, that Lincoln wrote the Gettysburg Address on a "rough sheet of foolscap" with a pencil while en route from the White House to the dedication ceremonies.

The moral is that Arnold's *Life*, like nearly every other early biography, should be used with caution. After all, the persistent research of the last quarter-century has produced results. Modern scholarship has not cast doubt on the cardinal features of Lincoln's character nor undermined the greatness of his achievements, but it has corrected many details in the record of his life. —Which is to say that in spite of Arnold's clear and readable style, in spite of the high standing of his book sixty years ago, his *Life of Abraham Lincoln* is valuable today chiefly for his own comments and impressions.

FRANCIS FISHER BROWNE.
THE EVERY-DAY LIFE OF ABRAHAM LINCOLN. 1886 and 1913.

In 1886 Francis Fisher Browne, already well known in literary circles as editor of *The Dial*, brought out a new kind of Lincoln biography. Essentially, it was a collection of anecdotes and reminiscences by men who had known Lincoln, woven by the author into a continuous narrative. Some of those who were quoted were established biographers like Holland, Lamon, Arnold, and J. H. Barrett; others—Herndon, Nicolay, and Hay—would soon be famous; still others, even then only minor luminaries, are now forgotten except by close students of the period. Altogether, the author drew on more than five hundred sources.

The first edition of the *Every-Day Life of Abraham Lincoln* is valuable chiefly as an anthology and source book. Many of the sources on which Browne drew are well known and readily accessible; others are so obscure that they would be difficult to locate even in a large and well cataloged Lincoln collection; still others were contributed at the author's request, and are not in print except in his book. Throughout, the emphasis is on Lincoln's personality, which Browne thought had been inadequately portrayed in the books then available.

Three defects make the first edition less valuable than it might be. In the first place, there is a lack of careful integration, especially in the latter part of the book. As a result, the narrative is sometimes little more than a succession of anecdotes. Secondly, Browne did not evaluate or appraise his material once he had decided to include it. In the third place, although he usually named and identified his contributors, he did not indicate where their recollections, if in print, could be found. The reader, therefore, has to exercise his own critical faculty under a handicap, and is deprived of the opportunity of consulting easily a reminiscence which may have more for his purpose than Browne printed.

One of these defects—the lack of integration—was largely eliminated in the second edition of the *Every-Day Life*, which Browne completed only a month before his death in 1913. Although he added some new material, he reduced the size of the book by about a third, rewrote it thoroughly, and gave it a far greater degree of coherence than it originally possessed. The second edition, therefore, has genuine merit as a biography in addition to its value as a source book. The student interested in as much first-hand material as he can locate will continue to use the first edition, of which there are several issues; the general reader will find the revised edition more to his liking.

WILLIAM H. HERNDON AND JESSE W. WEIK.
  HERNDON'S LINCOLN: THE TRUE STORY
  OF A GREAT LIFE. 1889.

No sooner had Lincoln died than William H. Herndon, his law partner for many years, began to collect material for a biography. In Kentucky and Indiana he visited the regions where Lincoln had lived and interviewed old residents who had known the family; in Illinois he began taking statements from Lincoln's old friends who were accessible and opened correspondence with those who lived at a distance.

For awhile he worked so assiduously that he was able to render material assistance to Lincoln's early biographers—which he did willingly—and to deliver three lectures in the winter of 1865–66 and a fourth a year later.[7] Then his perseverance waned. His fourth lecture—that on Ann Rutledge—had stirred up a cloud of critics, he was worried by failing finances, and he was lapsing into occasional spells of intemperance. In 1869 he sold copies of the material he had collected to Ward Hill Lamon. For some time after the publication of Lamon's *Lincoln* he played with the idea of a

[7]The first three lectures were only recently printed in full. They may be found in the *Abraham Lincoln Quarterly* for September, 1941; December, 1941; and December, 1944. The fourth lecture, which was devoted in the main to Lincoln's romance with Ann Rutledge, was printed contemporaneously as a broadside. It was reprinted in 1910 by H. E. Barker and again in 1945 by the Trovillion Private Press.

collaboration with Chauncey F. Black, Lamon's embittered co-author, but nothing eventuated. As the years passed, the possibility of a biography by Lincoln's closest personal and professional associate became more and more remote.

Then Herndon met a younger man, Jesse W. Weik of Greencastle, Indiana, who was planning to write a series of magazine articles on Lincoln. He liked him, and with customary generosity poured out his own knowledge in long letters. By 1886 the projected magazine articles had become the long-promised biography, which Weik was to write from materials supplied by Herndon.[8] Herndon placed all his material in Weik's hands, visited him in Greencastle, and showered him with letters from Springfield. Weik worked rapidly, with the result that the book was finished late in 1888 and published in the following year.

Almost at once *Herndon's Lincoln* became the center of a controversy which has never ended. The basic issue has, however, shifted perceptibly with the years. Herndon's contemporary critics saw little reason for challenging his accuracy. Their concern was with a code of ethics which permitted him to reveal, and even emphasize, what they thought should have remained unrevealed. Present-day criticism, on the other hand, tends to ignore questions of propriety, but takes sharp exception to Herndon's factual accuracy in several important particulars.

Soon after publication, discussion crystallized about several features of Herndon's narrative, and these same features remain the principal points of contention. Readers were shocked—and some still are—by his assertion that

[8]Many of the letters from Herndon to Weik are included in *The Hidden Lincoln*.

Lincoln's mother was illegitimate. Few were disposed to doubt the essential facts of his account of Lincoln's romance with Ann Rutledge, but many looked upon publication of the story, and especially the inferences he drew from it, as a cruel indignity which Mrs. Lincoln should have been spared. His melodramatic tale of Lincoln's marriage, and his emphasis upon discord in the domestic relations of the Lincolns, appeared to many to be both improper and malicious. And his contention that Lincoln was not an orthodox Christian was certain to arouse acrimonious dispute in an age which saw the devil's wiles in Ingersoll's mild and flowery skepticism.

Many modern students have attacked all these features of *Herndon's Lincoln* from the standpoint of historical accuracy, and have sought to discredit the author by means of independent evidence. But for every challenger there has been a defender. Neither side has been clearly victorious, but it cannot be far wide of the mark to chalk up the score to date about as follows:

In the matter of the illegitimacy of Lincoln's mother, the preponderance of evidence favors Herndon. However, many documents are missing, and it is not impossible that this conclusion will someday be reversed.

Herndon's account of the Ann Rutledge romance is too highly colored. That there was a romance can hardly be doubted, but there is no good reason for believing that Ann Rutledge was the only woman Lincoln ever loved, as Herndon insisted, and that her death affected him throughout his life.

The story of Lincoln's failure to appear for his wedding is

no longer tenable, and Herndon's account of the domestic difficulties of the Lincolns is overdrawn, though not baseless.

The presentation of Lincoln's religious opinions is unsatisfactory in two respects: terminology is not clear, and is therefore susceptible of misunderstanding; and no account is taken of the deepening of Lincoln's belief under the stress of war.

In one other particular, which was not a matter of original controversy, present-day students have corrected Herndon. They have shown conclusively that Lincoln's childhood and youth were not spent in grinding, degrading poverty, nor was his father the worthless vagrant the author pictured. On the other hand, the environment was not on the high level some enthusiasts have imagined. The truth seems to be that Lincoln was born into and brought up in typical pioneer surroundings.

These matters take up only a small part of the book. One may write them all off, and still have a biography that must be included in any Lincoln shelf. For twenty years Herndon was closer to Lincoln than anyone except his wife, and far earlier than most, he sensed his partner's potential greatness. He was an accurate observer; he had a good memory; and he could make a vivid phrase. In biographical creed he was a realist, adamantly resolved to give posterity the man he had known rather than an embodiment of the myth he believed the sentimentalists were creating. These qualities, with Weik's considerable literary skill, resulted in a book that makes a lasting impression on every reader. Here, one feels, is Lincoln as he actually appeared in his law office, on Springfield's streets, in the courts of the old eighth circuit,

and at dozens of Illinois political meetings. One laughs at
his ribald but hilarious stories, or steps softly for fear of
breaking into his brooding melancholy. If this is not the
real Lincoln, then it is a great work of artistic imagination.
And nothing we know about Herndon or Weik indicates
that either was capable of sheer creation on this level.

It is the real Lincoln, but not the whole Lincoln. Four-
fifths of the book is devoted to the period before 1861.
Lincoln's administration is covered sketchily. The reader
would do well to remember that Herndon knew nothing at
first hand of the period of Lincoln's greatest growth, and
make his own allowances for the effect of this lacuna on
many of his judgments.[9]

No sooner had *Herndon's Lincoln* appeared than rumors
began to circulate to the effect that Robert Lincoln was
attempting to "suppress" the book by purchasing every
available copy. The story still receives wide credence, although it appears to be untrue.[10] The relative scarcity of
the biography may be accounted for by the fact that the
publishers, Belford, Clarke & Co. of Chicago, failed soon
after the book appeared. Scribner's wanted to buy the copyright and bring out a new edition, but under pressure—
seemingly from Robert Lincoln—the firm withdrew in

[9]A more detailed appraisal of *Herndon's Lincoln* is to be found in the preface to my
edition, published by Albert & Charles Boni in 1930. William E. Barton presented
the best case against the legitimacy of Lincoln's mother in his *Life of Abraham Lincoln*.
Louis A. Warren has developed the other side of the argument in many publications,
but most concisely in *The Lincoln Kinsman* for August, 1938, October, 1938, April,
1940, and March, 1941. For a critique of Herndon's story of Lincoln's marriage, see
Sandburg and Angle, *Mary Lincoln, Wife and Widow*, Appendix. This same book offers a balanced account of domestic life in the Lincoln family. Lincoln's religion has
been the subject of dozens of books and pamphlets. All relevant evidence on the
question is conveniently accessible in William E. Barton, *The Soul of Abraham Lincoln*.
[10]See *The Hidden Lincoln*, 238, 244, 249, 261.

favor of D. Appleton & Co. Appleton printed a revised edition under Horace White's editorship in 1892, and has kept it in print ever since. In the revised edition less than two pages of the original were deleted, while White added a valuable chapter on the Lincoln-Douglas debates of 1858.

NICOLAY AND HAY.
ABRAHAM LINCOLN: A HISTORY. 1890.

Long before the end of Lincoln's administration his young secretaries, John G. Nicolay and John Hay, decided to write the history of his life and times. To this end Nicolay made many notes, and Hay kept a diary. Lincoln knew of their intentions, and gave them his full co-operation. After his death, Robert Lincoln opened the President's papers to them, and furthered their undertaking by every means at his command.

The two men, however, had other responsibilities besides writing the Lincoln biography. Moreover, they had undertaken a large-scale work. It is not surprising, therefore, that more than twenty years passed before the first chapters were presented to the public. Then, in order that the largest possible number of readers might be reached, the biography was serialized in the *Century Magazine*. Although not much more than half of the finished book was published in this way, its size was such that serial publication took more than three years. The whole work, in book form, filled ten sizable volumes.

The title—*Abraham Lincoln: A History*—indicates the nature of the book. The full subtitle, which now appears only on the dust wrapper, is even more descriptive: "A

History of the United States from the Birth of Lincoln to the Close of the Civil War." The book is, in fact, both biography and history. In the first volume Lincoln is the center of attention, but in the second the reader is introduced to the method followed throughout the remainder of the work: one or more chapters of history with little or no mention of Lincoln, and then a chapter or two in which he is the central figure.

The strictly biographical part of Nicolay and Hay has high merit. One who reads the book today soon comes to suspect that many of those who have written disparagingly of it either have never read it, or have read it so long ago that they have forgotten what it contains. Much has been made, for example, of the authors' deference to Robert Lincoln, of their acceptance of his censorship, and of the fact that theirs is the "official" biography. Nevertheless, one may read the simple, unelaborated, but unqualified statement that "Mrs. Lincoln's mother [that is, Nancy Hanks's mother] was named Lucy Hanks." In a biography heavily censored by the son of Mary Todd Lincoln the reader would hardly expect to find Ann Rutledge, but in Nicolay and Hay he will read that Lincoln was "much attached" to her, and "profoundly affected" by her death. The authors relate the story of Lincoln's courtship of Mary Owens, including the letter to Mrs. Browning in which he burlesqued the affair. Moreover, the near-duel with Shields, of which Lincoln himself was always ashamed, is described in detail.

The mature Lincoln, to be sure, is always presented in conventional terms. But, as Tyler Dennett has pointed out,[11] the authors themselves were conventional men. Their Lincoln, one feels sure, was shaped not so much by the restraining hand of Lincoln's son as by their own codes and convictions.

To the present-day reader, the book's greatest merit is that which is implied by the following passage in the authors' preface:

We knew Mr. Lincoln intimately before his election to the Presidency. We came from Illinois to Washington with him, and remained at his side and in his service—separately or together—until the day of his death. We were the daily and nightly witnesses of the incidents, the anxieties, the fears, and the hopes which pervaded the Executive Mansion and the National Capital. The President's correspondence, both official and private, passed through our hands; he gave us his full confidence. We had personal acquaintance and daily official intercourse with Cabinet Officers, Members of Congress, Governors, and Military and Naval Officers of all grades, whose affairs brought them to the White House. It was during these years of the war that we formed the design of writing this history and began to prepare for it. President Lincoln gave it his sanction and promised his cordial cooperation. After several years' residence in Europe, we returned to this country and began the execution of our long-cherished plan. Mr. Robert T. Lincoln gave into our keeping all the official and private papers and manuscripts in his possession, to which we have added all the material we could acquire by industry or by purchase. It is with the advantage, therefore, of a wide personal acquaintance with all the leading participants of the war, and of perfect familiarity with the manuscript material, and also with the assistance of the vast bulk of printed records and treatises which we have accumulated since 1865, that we have prosecuted this work to its close.

Much of the archival material upon which Nicolay and Hay relied is now in print. Nevertheless, it is a convenience to have it assembled in coherent order. Many of their

[11] *John Hay: From Poetry to Politics*, 141. Ch. XII of this book is devoted to the writing of *Abraham Lincoln: A History*.

sources, on the other hand, remain unavailable except in the form of the excerpts which they themselves published. This is true of letters to Lincoln, which only they have had the privilege of using,[12] of Nicolay's memoranda, of General Scott's daily reports to the President in April, 1861, and many other personal papers of almost equal importance.

In addition to the merit which the book derives from the documentary material incorporated in it, it has other good points. The first volume ranks high as a biographical narrative. The description of Illinois in the 'thirties, when Lincoln settled there, is excellent. The chapter on Lincoln's marriage is frank and perceptive—a better account, in most respects, than later biographers have achieved. Succeeding volumes contain many passages without which Lincoln biography would be much thinner than it is. Among these are the description of Lincoln's first inauguration, the account of the evolution of the first inaugural address, Lincoln's trials with office-seekers, and the sections which deal with the effect on him of the Fort Sumter crisis and other critical episodes in the course of the war. To these passages the first-hand knowledge of the authors imparted the quality of primary sources.

Considered as history, Nicolay and Hay is less satisfactory. Throughout, the book is colored by the irrefragable Republicanism of the authors. "It is now universally understood, if not conceded," they declared, "that the Rebellion of 1861 was begun for the sole purpose of defending and

---

[12]Presumably, all such letters are in the Lincoln collection now impounded in the Library of Congress. This collection is to be opened in 1947.

preserving to the seceding States the institution of African slavery and making them the nucleus of a great slave empire, which in their ambitious dreams they hoped would include Mexico, Central America, and the West India Islands, and perhaps even the tropical States of South America."[14] They could make this statement, and many others of similar tenor, and still believe that they were being completely objective, but to a later generation such asseverations are only indications of a partisanship which is proved by the text itself.

Partisanship, however, can easily be allowed for. Make the allowance, and Nicolay and Hay remains a book to reward both student and reader. For the former, there are documentary material and the first-hand testimony of authors who were themselves participants in the events of which they wrote; for the latter, a history of the Civil War unexcelled in comprehensiveness. This is one narrative that covers the whole great sweep of events—political developments, South as well as North; military campaigns, not only in the East but also in the often-neglected West and Southwest; the naval war; emancipation; military government and the problems it occasioned; foreign affairs; reconstruction; Lincoln's assassination and funeral. A fine chapter on Lincoln's fame serves as a conclusion.

Not the least merit of *Abraham Lincoln: A History* is the large number of illustrations and maps which it contains.

[14]I, 312.

IDA M. TARBELL.
THE LIFE OF ABRAHAM LINCOLN. 1900.

This is one of the most popular Lincoln biographies ever published. Between 1900 and 1928 at least eleven editions appeared, and even today the book has many readers.

That Tarbell's *Lincoln* should have a big sale was inevitable. In 1894 the author, a newcomer to the staff of *McClure's Magazine*, was given the assignment of locating men and women who had known Lincoln and writing a series of articles based on their reminiscences. The articles were well received. Made into a book—*The Early Life of Abraham Lincoln*—they won more readers. Encouraged by success, the editors of the magazine carried the series beyond Lincoln's early life, and thus made possible this full-length biography. When published, it fell into a market well prepared by long serialization.

But there were other reasons for the book's success. The frankly eulogistic point of view of the author was welcome to readers to whom Herndon's realism had been repulsive; her journalistic approach and relative brevity were in pleasing contrast to Nicolay and Hay's ten sober volumes of Civil War history. Miss Tarbell, moreover, challenged a number of Herndon's most controversial contentions, and adduced seemingly irrefutable evidence to support her arguments.

Here are the book's merits as the author saw them:

The new material collected will, we believe, add considerably to our knowledge of Lincoln's life. Documents are presented establishing clearly that his mother was not the nameless girl that she has been so generally believed. His father, Thomas Lincoln, is shown to have been something more than a shiftless "poor white," and Lincoln's early life, if hard and crude, to have been full of honest, cheerful effort at betterment. His struggles for a livelihood and his intellectual development from the time he started out for himself until he was admitted to the bar are traced with more detail than in any other biography, and considerable new light is thrown on this period of his life. The sensational account of his running away from his own wedding, accepted generally by historians, is shown to be false. To the period of Lincoln's life from 1849, when he gave up politics, until 1858, the period of the Lincoln and Douglas Debates, the most important contribution made is the report of what is known as the "Lost Speech." [15]

Nearly half a century later, few students would accept Miss Tarbell's claims in their entirety. As has been pointed out,[16] the question of the legitimacy of Lincoln's mother is still an open one, and even those who agree with Miss Tarbell's conclusion find it necessary to make a number of corrections in her argument. It is now generally conceded that the story of Lincoln's failure to appear at his wedding is without foundation, but it was not until many years after Tarbell's *Lincoln* that a convincing reconstruction of Lincoln's marriage was published.[17] Whitney's version of the "Lost Speech," moreover, now appears to be a sheer fabrication. On the other hand, Miss Tarbell and others have succeeded in establishing Thomas Lincoln on a somewhat higher social and economic level, and in the perspective of time Lincoln's early life appears less drab than it did to his first biographers.

Considered historically—looked at as a step in the gradual perfecting of the story of Lincoln's life—Miss Tarbell's

[15]Preface, ix.
[16]See p. 30.
[17]See p. 110.

Life of Abraham Lincoln is important for two reasons. In the first place, by emphasizing the personal, and by stressing Lincoln's life prior to the presidency, it drew the interest of hundreds of thousands of readers from what he had done to what he was, and deepened their understanding of him as a man. In the second place, it brought to light and preserved many reminiscences which otherwise would have been lost.

Today, only the second claim to distinction endures. The human qualities of Abraham Lincoln are so generally known and so fully appreciated that no one needs to read Tarbell to be made aware of them. Besides, there are better biographies—better in factual accuracy, proportion, and profundity. But the recollections which Miss Tarbell gathered remain. True, in her pages they are rarely documented or fully identified, many have since been published elsewhere, and many have to be used with caution; but their availability in her work is still something for which close students of Lincoln's life must be grateful.

In the *Life of Abraham Lincoln* Miss Tarbell included nearly 200 pages of Lincoln letters, telegrams, and documents which were not then to be found in Nicolay and Hay's *Complete Works of Abraham Lincoln*. Since 1900 all the important items in this section of the book have been included in the various supplemental compilations of Lincoln's writings,[18] but many of the telegrams can still be found here only.

[18]See Part One of this work.

JOHN G. NICOLAY.
A SHORT LIFE OF ABRAHAM LINCOLN. 1902.

The subtitle of this biography indicates that it is a condensation of Nicolay and Hay's ten-volume work. However, it has character of its own. Only in proportion and scope does it resemble *Abraham Lincoln: A History*. Like that book, it is concerned primarily with Lincoln's administration, and the story of the presidency which it offers is largely a history of the Civil War.

Except for the initial chapters, in which the narrative hugs Lincoln's own letters and speeches, the *Short Life* reminds one of a first-rate encyclopedia article expanded to 550 pages. That characterization is not intended to be derogatory, for a first-rate encyclopedia article has many merits. The style is likely to be dry, but a high degree of objectivity, and broad coverage, are usually met with. So it is with Nicolay's *Short Life*. In it are to be found excellent summaries of all the major problems of the war and Lincoln's attitude towards them—military affairs, slavery and emancipation, political divisions and differences, the election of 1864, reconstruction, the attempts of Greeley, Blair, and others to make peace between North and South, the final defeat of the Confederacy.

The reader who wants a comprehensive account of Lincoln's life and times in one average-sized volume can do no better than this. The book deserves to be better known and more widely read.

Lord Charnwood.

ABRAHAM LINCOLN. 1916.

In 1917, when the first American edition of this book appeared, the United States had just entered a war in which the issue, as men then saw it, was the survival of democracy. How did Lincoln, the personification of the democratic ideal, appear against this new and terrible background? In an answer offered by an Englishman there was bound to be wide interest.

The continuing popularity of Charnwood's *Lincoln*, however, cannot be accounted for by its initial timeliness. Only basic qualities can keep a book alive year after year, especially when its subject is one in which new interpretations appear at short intervals.

In the case of Charnwood the characteristics that continue to attract readers become evident from even a casual reading. When the book is compared to other biographies, they stand out clearly.

In the first place, it is not primarily factual, as for example, Nicolay's *Short Life* is factual. The emphasis is rather upon interpretation and analysis. It is significant that Charnwood should cover one of the critical periods of Lincoln's career—the four years that intervened between his political re-awakening in 1854 and his challenge to Douglas in 1858—in six pages, and then devote fifteen pages to a careful and detailed analysis of his position on what was to be the principal issue of the ensuing contest— the political aspects of the slavery question. To Charnwood, the center of interest was always what kind of man Lincoln was. Facts he used only in so far as they illuminated this focal question.

Charnwood saw Lincoln as a character exceedingly complex and by no means fully understood. The President's "greatness of mind and heart" he took to be amply demonstrated. What interested him, as interpreter, far more strongly were the major decisions and acts of Lincoln's administration. "Hardly an action of his Presidency is exempt from controversy," he wrote. It was his intention, therefore, to examine carefully "just those actions and just those qualities of his upon which candid detraction has in fact fastened, or on which candid admiration has pronounced with hesitancy."

One finds, therefore, full discussion of secession and Lincoln's attitude towards it; of his relations with his cabinet and his commanders, especially McClellan; of his moulding of opinion and his efforts to keep the North unified; of slavery and emancipation; and of the basic principles which, in his mind, were the only possible justification of the carnage. The discussion, moreover, is not Socratic, for Charnwood did not hesitate to express judgments, and they were not always laudatory. Permeating the book, however, is the author's conviction that Lincoln was one of the world's truly great men—that he was a man "quite unlike the many statesmen whom power and the vexations attendant upon it have in some piteous way spoiled and marred, a man who started by being tough and shrewd and canny and became very strong and very wise, started with an inclination to honesty, courage, and kindness, and became, under a tremendous strain, honest, brave, and kind to an almost tremendous degree."[19]

In the second place, Charnwood clarified the story of Lincoln's life by including many passages devoted to straight American history or to explanations of the American political system. The second chapter is a summary of American history from the Revolutionary War to 1830; throughout the book there are numerous shorter interpolations. A native author assumes that his readers are already familiar with these matters; Charnwood, writing for Englishmen, realized that explanation was essential. The probability is, of course, that the average American is not much better informed about his country's history and institutions than the average Englishman, and therefore he also welcomes an elementary introduction to those subjects.

Finally, Charnwood brought literary skill to the Lincoln theme. Nicolay, by himself, was prosaic. John Hay could write, but in collaboration with Nicolay he purposely throttled his stylistic individuality. Miss Tarbell's work was journalism, hastily written and without distinction. The Lincoln centennial inspired a flood of books and articles, but none blended substantive and literary merit. Charnwood, on the other hand, wrote prose marked by clarity and a fine sense of proportion. In Lincoln biography, those qualities were something of a novelty.

NATHANIEL W. STEPHENSON.
LINCOLN. 1922.

Within five years a one-volume biography by an American, Nathaniel W. Stephenson, rivalled Charnwood's

[19]P. 238.

Lincoln in popularity. The book had rare literary charm, while its Freudian overtones appealed to a reading public then much occupied with the subconscious. Moreover, it dealt largely with the political aspects of Lincoln's administration, and in 1922 that was a subject to which Woodrow Wilson's recent experiences had given unusual timeliness.

Today, Stephenson's excursions into psychoanalysis seem thin and unconvincing. One who reads that Lincoln's desolation after Ann Rutledge's death was "his mother reborn in him," that "it was all the shadowiness of his mother's world; all that frantic reveling in the mysteries of woe to which, hitherto, her son had been an alien," is likely only to shrug his shoulders; and when he is informed that Lincoln's faith in a mighty government which should use its power with solicitous restraint came "out of the shadowy parts of him, beyond the limits of his or any man's conscious vision, dim, unexplored, but real and insistent as those forest recesses from which his people came," he will probably indulge in a more emphatic gesture of disbelief.

Equally unconvincing is Stephenson's theory of the ebb and flow of Lincoln's will power. From 1849 until 1862, when he reached a permanent plateau of self-mastery, he alternated between moods of depression and confidence. So said Stephenson. His lapses, moreover, were largely attributable to his father, "Thomas the unstable," whose ghost was a force "to be reckoned with in his son's life" during this period!

What does hold up is Stephenson's account of Lincoln's presidency, to which four-fifths of the book is devoted. Like

Charnwood, he was interested in explaining Lincoln's springs of action rather than in narrating the facts of his life. In the Civil War President he saw two great achievements: the making of a strong nation, and the tempering of that strength with tolerance, justice, and high moral quality. To trace these achievements from germ to fruition it was essential that he look at Lincoln's administration from one focal point only—the White House. His center of interest never shifts. Military events, taking place at a distance, are summarized in a sentence or two, but the political struggle for the control of the army is related at length. About domestic politics in the country at large Stephenson cared little; what interested him was the long tug between Lincoln and the politicians, mostly members of his own party, on Capitol Hill. Parts of the story—those which deal with Lincoln's basic political philosophy, his religion, emancipation, reconstruction, his second election—have never been better told within a single volume.

Stephenson's *Lincoln* is a fine complement to the *Short Life* of John G. Nicolay. In the one are all the facts of Lincoln's presidency, succinctly presented; in the other is the story of Lincoln's effort to keep the power of the government in his own hands, not for personal or partisan ends, but in order that the nation might emerge united, strong, and good.

WILLIAM E. BARTON.
    THE LIFE OF ABRAHAM LINCOLN. 1925.

"He who adds another to the already long list of biographies of Abraham Lincoln should be ready to give a

reason for the faith that is within him." Thus wrote the
Rev. William E. Barton in the Introduction to his *Life of
Abraham Lincoln.* "My reasons," he added, "are three":

> The first is that the biographies of Lincoln already in print have not
> discovered all the important facts of his life. Their authors have shown,
> in the main, commendable diligence, and I am greatly indebted to my
> predecessors; but I have been able to explore with greater thorough-
> ness some fields hitherto inadequately covered and to penetrate some
> areas hitherto unknown . . . .
>
> The second reason is that all of the extant biographies of Lincoln
> contain inaccuracies, some of them trivial, others important, and a few
> of them very grave. I am able to correct some of these errors and I hope
> that I am not adding any new ones.
>
> The third reason is that it is now possible to write a life of Lincoln
> with a perspective of more than half a century. Contemporaries are
> valuable witnesses but notoriously incompetent judges.

The two good-sized volumes of Barton's *Life* bear convincing testimony to the accuracy of the first of these claims.
The early chapters added a great deal to the existing body
of knowledge about the Lincoln and Hanks families and
placed that knowledge on a sound documentary foundation. The author's most sensational contribution was a
demonstration that Nancy Hanks was the natural daughter
of Lucy Hanks—a demonstration which, if not conclusive,
was so cogently presented, and accompanied by so much
circumstantial evidence, that most students continue to
accept it. Barton was the first biographer to make use of the
diary of Orville H. Browning, to reveal William H. Townsend's findings regarding the law suits in which Lincoln was
a principal, to tell the story of Lincoln's ownership of a
Springfield German-language newspaper, and to draw on
Elizabeth Todd Grimsley's account of the first weeks of the

Lincoln family in the White House.[20] And his account of Lincoln's Gettysburg Address was far superior to anything that had appeared up to that time.

Barton's second claim—that he had rectified many errors of his predecessors, and added few if any of his own—was also well founded, although his correctional contribution was much less important than his positive one. In perspective (his third justification) he showed no perceptible advance over Charnwood and Stephenson.

For these merits, however, a price was demanded of the reader. Barton's account of the Lincoln and Hanks families is characterized by such great detail that something perilously close to tedium results. His own interest in this and other subjects where he made important contributions— notably the Gettysburg Address—threw the narrative badly out of proportion. He was often discursive; his comments about his predecessors in the field of Lincoln study were frequently uncharitable; his self-commendation became tiresome.

Moreover, much of the book—most, one might say, of the second volume—is undistinguished. The *Welles Diary*, *McClellan's Own Story*, the diary of John Hay, Lincoln's own writings, and a relatively small number of other well known sources provided him with most of his material. One has only to compare Barton's *Life*—always excepting those

---

[20] *The Diary of Orville Hickman Browning, 1850-1881*, Theodore C. Pease and James G. Randall, editors, has since been published as Volumes 20 and 22 (1927 and 1933) of The Illinois Historical Collections (The Illinois State Historical Library, Springfield). William H. Townsend's research was published in his *Abraham Lincoln Defendant* (Houghton Mifflin, Boston, 1923), and *Lincoln the Litigant* (Houghton Mifflin, Boston, 1925). Elizabeth Todd Grimsley's "Six Months in the White House" may be found in the *Journal* of the Illinois State Historical Society for April, 1926.

portions which constitute notable contributions—with a book like James G. Randall's *The Civil War and Reconstruction* to be made acutely aware that much of it is decidedly superficial.[21]

Barton's *Life*, nevertheless, retains importance for the serious student. It is still the best source for the ancestry of Lincoln, both maternal and paternal, and the several essays which form the conclusion of the book—"Lincoln and Labor," "Lincoln the Orator," "The Humor of Abraham Lincoln," "Mrs. Lincoln," and "Mr. Lincoln"—continue to reward careful reading.

CARL SANDBURG.
ABRAHAM LINCOLN: THE PRAIRIE YEARS. 1926.

This biography stands alone. If the word "incomparable" be given its literal meaning, only this book among the thousands which deal with the life of Lincoln deserves it. Although its author, prior to publication, was known chiefly as a poet, *The Prairie Years* and its sequel[22] have made him the most famous of modern biographers. With *The War Years*, it is the longest Lincoln biography. Nevertheless, it is safe to say that it has been read by more people, and has done more to make Lincoln a living figure in readers' minds, than any other contribution to Lincolniana.

A large part of the appeal of *The Prairie Years* comes from the fact that Carl Sandburg is a very great artist with

[21]Barton's posthumous *President Lincoln* is already deservedly forgotten.
[22]*Abraham Lincoln: The War Years.* See pp. 56–58.

words. Consider, for example, the poetry of the following passage:

The mother of Nancy was nineteen years old when she made this trip, leaving Nancy's father, who had not married her, back in Virginia. She could croon in the moist evening twilight to the shining face in the sweet bundle, "Hush thee, hush thee, thy father's a gentleman." She could toss the bundle into the air against a far, hazy line of blue mountains, catch it in her two hands as it came down, let it snuggle to her breast and feed, while she asked, "Here we come—where from?"

And after they had both sunken in the depths of forgetful sleep, in the early dark and past midnight, the tug of a mouth at her nipples in the gray dawn matched in its freshness the first warblings of birds and the morning stars leaving the earth to the sun and the dew.

Or of this:

Joshua Speed was a deep-chested man of large sockets, with broad measurement between the ears. A streak of lavender ran through him; he had spots soft as May violets. And he and Abraham Lincoln told each other their secrets about women. Lincoln too had tough physical shanks and large sockets, also a streak of lavender, and spots soft as May violets.

Or, in a different mood, this:

The trains into Springfield unloaded hundreds of passengers on a single day, arriving to see Lincoln. . . . They said they nominated and elected him President, and inquired about post offices, revenue collectorships, clerkships, secretaryships. They wore him. Behind their smiles some had snouts like buzzards, pigs, rats. They were pap-seekers, sapsuckers, chair-warmers, hammock heroes, the office-sniffing mob who had killed Zach Taylor, who had killed Tippecanoe Harrison. They wore Lincoln—worse than the signs of war.

Many a reader, moreover, is drawn by the dual character of *The Prairie Years*—by the author's success in telling the story of Lincoln's life, and at the same time depicting a series of shifting panoramas of the United States of Lincoln's time. One finds here a whole people—the "half horse, half alligator" men of the rivers, the gamblers of the packets and water fronts from Louisville to Natchez, scala-wag lawyers and backwoods hunters, slave owners and slave dealers. One gets glimpses of raw new factories in Europe as well as in the United States; one sees the little railroad engines, puffing yearly over more and more miles of track. There are pictures of the great plantations of the South and of the growing cities of the North—the mill towns of New England, the prairie capital of Springfield, Chicago feeling the burgeoning strength of its muscles as it plays host to the Republican National Convention of 1860. These and hundreds of other pictures, incidents, trends in the making of a nation introduce most readers to a kind of history they never suspected could be written.

The Prairie Years has another quality, and one that is hard to define. Call it lifelikeness. That is to say that Sandburg lived with a man of another time so intimately and over so many years that the man long dead became fully alive in his mind. And because of his gift of words—because he could make them convey images, meanings, and thoughts with a rare degree of effectiveness—he succeeded in cre-ating the same illusion of reality in the minds of millions of readers.

So much the most severe critic is bound to admit. He will, however, point out that there are other qualities of *The Prairie Years* that must be mentioned in any thoroughgoing appraisal. Prominent among them is Sandburg's propen-sity to make his imagination serve in place of orthodox historical evidence. When, for example, he writes of young Lincoln steering a flatboat down the Mississippi in 1828 and asserts that "the personality and the ways of Andrew Jackson filled his thoughts," and that "he asked himself many questions and puzzled his head about the magic of this one strong, stormy man filling the history of that year," the hard-headed critic can reply that Sandburg knows no more about what Lincoln was thinking at that time than he knows about his life after death. In neither case is there any record. When Sandburg writes that "the name 'Ann Rutledge' would come to him and he would pronounce it softly to the shadows in the blacksmith shop where he lay burning wood shavings to light the pages of Kirkham's Grammar"—and this is only one of many such averments— one may ask, legitimately, for the evidence. And there is nothing but the author's own creative power.

The critic is also likely to point out that *The Prairie Years* is often discursive, even formless; that all sorts of odds and ends of information—Sandburg's "elusive outlines of the civilization of the United States"—bear little relation to the main theme; that many a biographical sketch several pages in length—of Harriet Beecher Stowe, for example, or Hinton Rowan Helper, or Ralph Waldo Emerson, or Walt Whitman—is on the far periphery of Lincoln's life; that anecdotes strung along for page after page become tiresome; and that many details are inaccurate.[23]

In refutation whereof the reader is likely to retort in the words of H. L. Mencken: "Are the facts all respected? Is the narrative satisfactory to the professors of Lincolology? To hell with the professors of Lincolology!"[24]

[23]Should the reader be interested in adverse criticism, he will find it set forth at length by Milo M. Quaife in a review which appeared in the *Mississippi Valley Historical Review* for September, 1926, 287–91.

[24]*The American Mercury*, July, 1926, 382. "Lincolology" appears to be one of Mr. Mencken's many contributions to the American language.

ALBERT J. BEVERIDGE.
ABRAHAM LINCOLN, 1809–1858. 1928.

When Albert J. Beveridge finished his *Life of John Marshall* he began almost at once to gather material for a biography of Lincoln. Both books, in his plan, were to be parts of an institutional interpretation of the United States which would begin with colonial times and end with the close of the Civil War. He attacked the task with the energy that was one of his most striking personal characteristics. He accepted nothing on faith, but insisted on verifying his sources, no matter how often they had been used by previous writers. He made repeated journeys to the Lincoln country. He worked tirelessly in the newspaper files of a dozen libraries. And he examined collection after collection of unpublished manuscripts.

Having finally assembled all the material he needed for a given subject, he reduced it to narrative form. Usually he revised each chapter several times before he was even reasonably well satisfied with it. Then it was mimeographed. In this form it was sent to scholars—often as many as twenty-five or thirty—who were urged to respond with the frankest and fullest criticism. After their comments were received and digested, the final rewriting took place.

Probably no scholar—certainly no Lincoln scholar—has ever tried harder to produce a definitive biography. But sometimes the affairs of men are disposed of with especial irony. So it was with Albert J. Beveridge. Sudden death, at the age of sixty-four, cut him off before he had finished the story of the Lincoln-Douglas debates, and before he had given his completed manuscript the final revision which was an essential part of his method. Moreover, Worthington C. Ford, who prepared the manuscript for publication, was enjoined from making any changes in the text beyond the correcting of obvious errors.

And so the Beveridge *Lincoln* missed definitiveness. But even if death had not intervened, it is clear that the book would not have attained this mirage-like goal. Research since Beveridge's time has indicated the need for considerable revision. Most present-day students would agree that his characterization of Thomas Lincoln is too severe and his picture of the Kentucky period of Lincoln's life too drab; that his story of Lincoln's courtship and broken engagement follows the Herndon account too closely; that his interpretation of Lincoln's share in the writing of the "Rebecca" letters (which led to the near-duel with Shields) is faulty; that his account of the Peoria "truce" with Douglas in 1854 is in error; and that Whitney's report of Lincoln's "Lost Speech," which he accepted without reservations, deserves no confidence. And doubtless time will force still further modifications.

Having said this, one hastens to stress the fact that these are by no means fatal defects. On the contrary, Beveridge's *Lincoln* is biography of a high order. In the first place, Lincoln's life is placed in a full framework of national history. The first sentences foreshadow the author's method. In two pages Beveridge sketched the salient features of the Jefferson administration, then in power; alluded to the warring nations of Europe, where Napoleon was at the apex of his career, and concluded: "Far from the turmoil, across the mountains, in a log cabin in the heart of Kentucky, on February 12, 1809, Abraham Lincoln was born."

In the second place, long passages in the book stand as model treatments of their subjects. Beveridge's account of the Indiana period of Lincoln's life is unrivalled, though bitterly resented by Hoosier patriots. His is by long odds the best and most exhaustive treatment of Lincoln's eight years in the Illinois legislature, and of his one term in the national House of Representatives. In fact, Beveridge's account of Lincoln's entire political career, including party management as well as office holding, is unsurpassed, and not likely to be excelled. American party politics was a subject which Beveridge knew from beginning to end, and it is not surprising that he should have seen in Lincoln's political career many meanings to which other writers, lacking his intimate experience, have been blind.

In the third place, Beveridge did more than any other biographer to restore Stephen A. Douglas to his rightful place as an able, patriotic American, and a worthy rival of Lincoln. In fact, if one were to rely solely on the evidence of the Beveridge *Lincoln*, one might easily conclude that Douglas was the author's hero. Temperamentally, Douglas and Beveridge were far closer than Lincoln and Beveridge, and the results of this natural affinity are often evident. There is good reason for believing, however, that if Beveridge had lived long enough even to bring the narrative to Lincoln's first election, Lincoln would have stood out as the greater of the two men, though not at Douglas's cost.[25]

[25] This is my own inference from numerous conversations with Beveridge. Several others who knew him well support it.

These qualities, with the author's utilization of an enormous body of source material and elaborate documentation, make the book indispensable.

CARL SANDBURG.
ABRAHAM LINCOLN: THE WAR YEARS. 1939.

The four volumes of this work include well over one million words and make a book longer, by the size of a full-length novel, than all Lincoln's published speeches and writings; and longer, by an even greater margin, than the complete works of Shakespeare or the Holy Bible.

To evaluate a performance of such magnitude in three or four pages is impossible. Even the attempt calls for more assurance, more temerity even, than should characterize authors of surveys like this. All that one can do within the space available is to call attention to certain respects in which *The War Years* differs from *The Prairie Years*,[26] and refer the reader to *The Lincoln of Carl Sandburg*, the 48-page booklet in which the publishers brought together seven of the most penetrating reviews which the book elicited.

First, then, *The War Years* is infinitely larger in its scope and infinitely more detailed than its predecessor. To be sure, it covers only four years of Lincoln's life, but at the same time, it covers a nation. Here is the contemporary picture and opinion of Lincoln—how he looked to thousands of people of his own time and what they said about him—sifted and cemented by a biographer perfectly qualified, by temperament and long years of research, for his task. Here also are pictures of hundreds of other actors in

[26]See p. 49.

the great drama of a nation in civil war—men and women whose names are household words even today, many others long forgotten. Altogether, the book is an incredibly complex compendium.

The word "compendium," though not strictly accurate, is used purposely. Much of *The War Years* is quotation—not from other scholars, but from Lincoln's contemporaries. In a sense, it is a gigantic piece of reporting, with relatively little probing on the part of the author for causes and trends. The effect on a reader accustomed to the neat analyses of orthodox historians is at first confusing. Gradually, however, he comes to realize that clear-cut explanations of human phenomena like the American Civil War are divinations of long afterward, and that the confusion of Sandburg's crowded pages is the confusion of the scene itself.

In *The War Years*, unlike *The Prairie Years*, Sandburg is wholly objective. Nowhere, in the later book, does he ascribe thoughts to Lincoln or to anyone else except on the basis of good evidence. All that the "professional" historians can criticize here is that he may have given more weight to this source and less to that than they would have done. And their criticisms—historians being notoriously individualistic—are not likely to be very convincing.

Perhaps because of its subject matter, perhaps by the author's design, *The War Years* is far less lyrical than the earlier book. There are passages, however, of sombre beauty unsurpassed. Many reviewers have been moved by the final chapter, in which the Lincoln funeral is described; others, myself included, have been more deeply stirred by the requiem, only a page in length, to the dead of Gettysburg.[27]

If the reader of this commentary has already read what has been written of *The Prairie Years*, he needs only to be reminded that that appraisal ended with a taunt ("to hell with the professors of Lincolology!") thrown by a literary critic. It is significant that this review, if it may be called that, can close on a note of praise by a great historian: "An air of grave thoughtfulness hangs over the lightest words. The searching, brooding spirit of the laborious historian pervades the treatment of every large problem. With this, that, and many things, specialists will doubtless quarrel more or less gently. . . . But when specialists have finished dissecting, scraping, refining, dissenting, and adding, I suspect that Mr. Sandburg's work will remain for long years to come a noble monument of American literature."[28]

JAMES G. RANDALL.
        LINCOLN THE PRESIDENT. 1945.

Not until twenty or twenty-five years ago did the "professional" historians[29] begin to pay much attention to the life of Lincoln. Then, for the most part, they confined themselves to the intensive study of limited phases of his career. Basing their work as closely as possible on documentary evidence, they have added many new facts and challenged many old conclusions. But by the very nature of their

[27]II, 476–77.
[28]Charles A. Beard in *The Virginia Quarterly Review*, Winter, 1940.
[29]The term requires definition. As used here, it signifies one who, after having taken advanced degrees in history, earns his living by teaching the subject, and subscribes to the accepted standards of the profession. Most important of these are resort to original sources, thorough documentation, and complete objectivity.

writings—by their disparate character and lack of popular appeal—they have had a smaller effect upon the prevailing conception of Lincoln than their efforts deserved. What has been needed is a synthesis, a comprehensive biography in which the findings of a generation of critical, professional scholars would be represented.

That, or something close to it, is what James G. Randall has supplied in *Lincoln the President*.[30] Although these two volumes carry the story only through Gettysburg—two more are promised—Lincoln's pre-presidential career is treated in considerable detail, and his character and personality are carefully delineated. Thus the scope of the book is much greater than its title indicates.

Revisionist conclusions are evident throughout. While following Herndon's interpretation of Lincoln's character in general, Randall rejects or qualifies several of his sensational contributions—notably the Ann Rutledge romance, his version of Lincoln's marriage, his harsh characterization of Mrs. Lincoln. Randall considers the Republican agitation of the slavery question from 1854 to 1860, and by inference, Lincoln's part in it, largely opportunistic. Between the positions assumed by Lincoln and Douglas in the debates of 1858 he finds little fundamental difference. Politics, rather than principle, animated the Republicans in 1860, and political maneuvering of the most practical kind brought about Lincoln's nomination. Buchanan, in

[30]If it should be maintained that Nathaniel W. Stephenson antedated Randall by many years, I reply that while Stephenson was a professional historian in the occupational sense, he paid little attention to the accepted standards of the craft when he wrote his *Lincoln*. A much better case can be made for Albert J. Beveridge, who took second place to no academician in his passion for accuracy. But Beveridge was not a product of the graduate schools, nor did he earn his living from teaching or historical research. Thus he fails to qualify under my purposely narrow definition.

his opinion, should be credited with the exercise of far more wisdom and patriotism than it has been the fashion to attribute to him.

Randall's most significant departure from historical tradition is his conviction, ably argued, that the Civil War was tragically unnecessary. Historians, he maintains, have stressed elements of discord when they have written about American history from 1850 to 1861. Randall maintains that by a different selection of facts they could have represented that period as one of progress and peace. Had they so represented it, the general belief that war was inevitable might never have become rooted. Randall finds that Northern and Southern differences over slavery were not important enough to lead to war, and neither were cultural nor economic divergencies. The Civil War, in his considered opinion, was the result of a crisis psychology, whipped up by extremists both North and South who were only a small fraction of the nation. The great majority in both sections wanted union and peace, but through ineptitude and unconcern they allowed the radicals to take the reins and guide the country to disaster.

(From his close study of the Civil War, supplemented, no doubt, by the ample data provided by events occurring in his own lifetime, Randall arrives at a conclusion that will startle many readers. "One of the most colossal of misconceptions," he writes, "is the theory that fundamental motives produce war. The glaring and obvious fact is the artificiality of war-making agitation.")

Despite his conviction that war was foisted on the nation, Randall does not see how Lincoln, in the situation that faced him in April, 1861, could have avoided the resort to arms. Nevertheless, his course as commander-in-chief left much to be desired. Into the War Department he first put Cameron, whose record stank, and then the "arrogant and intriguing" Stanton who, in Randall's opinion, has long enjoyed a far greater reputation than he deserved. McClellan, whom Randall considers the North's greatest commander, Lincoln sacrificed to the radicals of his own party.

In spite of these and other mistakes and failures, Randall's Lincoln is essentially the same towering, compelling figure that the American people long ago made their foremost folk hero. His faith in democracy, his commonness, his high moral character—these and other long-accepted attributes are unimpaired. In addition, Randall imputes notable achievements to him—chiefly his moderating influence on the course of foreign affairs, his wise management of public opinion, and his sane, conservative approach to the many problems presented by slavery.

Except for the long preliminary delineation of Lincoln's character, Randall's biography is primarily concerned with the political aspects of Lincoln's presidency. Military matters get summary treatment, and there is little that deals with the purely personal side of Lincoln's life in the White House. Its other outstanding characteristic is the mark that it bears of the detached, analytical mind that produced it. Time after time Randall argues the evidence on both sides of a controversial question. Unlike so many of his colleagues, however, he usually comes to a clear-cut conclusion, for the passing of judgments on his subject's actions is, in his creed, one of a biographer's obligations.

Lincoln the President will probably never reach the huge audiences that the works of Tarbell, Charnwood, and Sandburg have enjoyed, but no serious student can afford to disregard it, and many thoughtful readers should find it richly rewarding.

JAMES DAUGHERTY.
ABRAHAM LINCOLN. 1943.

All the biographies in this section have been included because they have significance for the serious, mature student of Lincoln's life. There should be a place, however, for at least one book that can be enjoyed by a boy or girl as well as by a man. Such is James Daugherty's *Abraham Lincoln*.

Simply, briefly, but with the deep pride of a fellow-countryman, Daugherty tells the story of the backwoods boy who came to stand, in the eyes of millions, for human freedom. And he tells it well. Admiration never leads him into mawkishness or blinds him to the earthy qualities that tied Lincoln to the plain people of his time—and of ours. Simplicity, moreover, does not connote carelessness as to facts, as it so often does, nor juvenility. Daugherty's prose is marked by a muscular lyricism that calls up image after image—of winter in southwestern Indiana, when "the wolves of the North Wind moaned and clashed among the branches, and January blizzards buried the land under the deep, soft snow;" of the mud in the public square at Springfield, "deep, rich, and juicy;" of "the great right hand of Abraham . . . weary and numb with gripping the soft paws of the stuffed shirts and the high hats;" of Lincoln's speech after Lee's surrender—"a cool sweet wind of peace and promise blowing over the hot embers of unextinguished fires of hate."

But Daugherty, richly talented, did not need to depend on words for pictures. Forty lithographs, all marked with the same vigor that characterizes his writing, sharpen the narrative and add materially to the reader's comprehension and enjoyment.

PART THREE

Monographs and Special Studies

Ancestry and Parentage

WILLIAM E. BARTON.
THE LINEAGE OF LINCOLN. 1929.

H ERE, in one volume, is traced the history of the Lincoln
and Hanks families from the first known representatives to Abraham Lincoln. The Lincoln line is carried
back, with reasonable certainty, to Norfolk, England; somewhat less surely the first of the Hankses is identified as
Thomas Hanks, of Malmesbury, a soldier under Cromwell
who was shipped to Virginia during the Civil War.

Dr. Barton's study is at times irritatingly discursive, yet
it has substantial merits. In it is to be found everything that
can be said with assurance about the two main streams of
Lincoln's ancestry, including much that the author himself
discovered. It is also the fullest extant treatment of the
Hanks family. In this line there is plenty of conjecture, as
Dr. Barton readily admitted, but his hypotheses have stood
the test of time better than any which have been advanced
in contradiction. This part of the book is marked, of course,
by a full-dress presentation of the author's contention that
Nancy Hanks was the natural daughter of Lucy Hanks.

In addition to the strictly genealogical passages there is
a good chapter on the quality of the Lincoln stock, and
another on the Lincoln family of Hancock County, Illinois

—the descendants of Abraham Lincoln's uncle, Mordecai Lincoln. On the other hand, the chapter entitled, "Lincoln Was a Lee" is the kind of thing that makes a good many sober citizens laugh at genealogists.

An Appendix includes 135 pages of documents. There is also a critical bibliography.

WILLIAM E. BARTON.
THE PATERNITY OF ABRAHAM LINCOLN. 1920.

This is an exhaustive, critical examination of the allegation, widely current twenty-five years ago, "that Abraham Lincoln was an illegitimate child; that his mother, Nancy Hanks, either before or subsequent to her marriage with Thomas Lincoln, if indeed she was married to him, became the mother of a son whose father was other than Thomas Lincoln."

Dr. Barton investigated seven alleged paternities in detail; others were found to be too absurd to deserve serious consideration. With the seven, his method was to assemble all available evidence in support of each putative father, and then subject that evidence to searching scrutiny. In every instance, the alleged paternity was seen to rest on a factual basis which no fair-minded student could accept.

The Paternity of Abraham Lincoln is one of those rare books that deserve to be called definitive. Rumors of Lincoln's illegitimacy have not passed out of circulation completely, but they are encountered far less often, and receive far less credence, than was formerly the case. For this, Dr. Barton's work is primarily responsible.

MARION DEXTER LEARNED.
ABRAHAM LINCOLN: AN AMERICAN MIGRATION. 1909.

The author of this study, who was Professor of Germanic Languages and Literatures at the University of Pennsylvania when it was made, undertook to verify the belief, then common among Germans in the United States, that Abraham Lincoln was descended from a German family by the name of Linkhorn. He ended by establishing clearly the English origin of the family, and the line of descent from Samuel Lincoln, the weaver who came to Hingham, Massachusetts, in 1637, to Abraham Lincoln, the grandfather of the President.

Dr. Barton, who leaned heavily upon this book, characterized it as "a good piece of work." Its chief value, today, however, lies in the documents of which it is largely made up.

WALDO LINCOLN.
HISTORY OF THE LINCOLN FAMILY. 1923.

This thick volume, by a genealogist of note, is the record of the descendants of Samuel Lincoln to the year 1920. The relationships of literally thousands of people are traced. The index alone, in six-point type set in double columns, occupies 102 pages. Discussions of evidence, biographical sketches, and many documents are interspersed throughout the text. It is more compact than Barton's *Lineage*, and covers much more ground, but by its very nature it lacks the sequential arrangement that makes the other book easy to use.

Childhood

Louis A. Warren.
   LINCOLN'S PARENTAGE AND
   CHILDHOOD. 1926.

Here are embodied the results of the first thorough documentary investigation of the Kentucky period of Lincoln's life.[1] Dr. Warren thus summarized the extent of his inquiry:

> Less than a dozen duly authorized public documents referring to the Lincoln and Hanks families in Kentucky were available at the beginning of this effort. I have been able to gather . . . 550 court entries bearing the name of either Lincoln or Hanks. Aside from these records that give direct contact with the Lincoln and Hanks families in Kentucky, 1000 other documents have been compiled which submit information about the environment in which the Lincolns moved, or record the activities of the cognate families. Supplementing these extracts from legal papers, a vast amount of material has come to hand consisting of military certificates, tombstone inscriptions, church and school record books, personal papers, and the like.

From this material, Dr. Warren advanced the boundaries of Lincoln study no small distance. He established the date and place of death of Abraham Lincoln, the President's grandfather. He argued, with moderation, that Lucy Hanks, the mother of Nancy, was a widow at the time of her marriage to Henry Sparrow. He proved that Thomas Lincoln was domiciled in Elizabethtown, Kentucky, and presumably living with his wife, in May, 1808, when Abraham Lincoln must have been conceived. He proved that Abraham Lincoln was born on the farm where the Lincoln Birthplace Memorial now stands, that it was a tract of 300

[1]One of the crying needs of Lincoln literature is a study like this for the years when the Lincoln family lived in Indiana. In the absence of a reliable monographic account, the reader is referred to Beveridge, *Abraham Lincoln, 1809–1858*.

acres, and that the present cabin is the one in which the birth took place. He showed that in the thirty-four years of Thomas Lincoln's residence in Kentucky there was "not one black mark against his name," that he was a sober citizen of good repute in the communities in which he lived, and that the childhood environment of his son was not a squalid one. And in addition to these and other specific contributions, he drew a general picture of the social conditions that prevailed in the part of Kentucky in which the Lincolns lived.

Throughout the book there is close dependence upon original records, with little attempt at embellishment. This does not make for easy reading, but the book is not dull to anyone who knows the fascination that comes from close contact with the bed-rock foundations of history.

Chronology

HARRY E. PRATT.
    LINCOLN: 1809–1839. 1941.
HARRY E. PRATT.
    LINCOLN: 1840–1846. 1939.
BENJAMIN P. THOMAS.
    LINCOLN: 1847–1853. 1936.
PAUL M. ANGLE.
    LINCOLN: 1854–1861. 1933.

These four volumes constitute a day-by-day account of Lincoln's life from the day of his birth until March 4, 1861. During the early years Thomas Lincoln's activities are recorded, but in 1830 the record shifts to Lincoln himself, and remains there. Beginning with the year 1834, each page is divided into seven equal spaces, and those spaces for which no record exists are left blank. For the most part, the entries are based on rock-bottom sources—court records, legislative journals, contemporary newspapers, Lincoln's own writings and those of his contemporaries.

Taken together, these books are to Lincoln study what the steel frame of a skyscraper is to the finished structure. In any piece of historical research the student must work out his chronology early in the undertaking. If he fails to do so, serious inaccuracies or omissions are likely to result. Many of the errors that persisted in Lincoln biography year after year were due to the lack of a detailed chronology. Thus writers went on repeating that a long visit to Joshua Speed's home in Kentucky finally restored Lincoln to health after the physical and nervous collapse caused by his broken engagement, whereas the record shows that he was absent from Springfield little more than a month. Temperance crusaders bent on making Lincoln a prohibitionist claimed that he stumped the state of Illinois on behalf of the Maine Law throughout the spring of 1855, but the day-by-day books prove the claim to be baseless. One biographer after another repeated the tale of the Peoria truce of 1854 and Douglas's violation of it; the chronology, by showing that Lincoln spoke repeatedly after October 16, proves either that the whole story is myth, or that Lincoln must share with Douglas the guilt of breaking the agreement. And these are only a few examples of the chronology's corrective value.

These books have also been a most effective means of detecting forgeries. The high price of Lincoln autographs has been a strong temptation to men of facile pens and easy morals. But the forger's historical knowledge is rarely impeccable: almost never does he turn out a letter which cannot be labeled as spurious by one who knows where Lincoln was and what he was doing on most of the days of his adult life. In dozens of cases within the writer's knowledge a quick reference to this chronology has proved a letter or document to be a forgery, and caused it to be withdrawn from sale or discredited as a source.

But the value of these books goes beyond that of a device for testing the soundness of Lincoln biography and the genuineness of his autograph letters and documents. They make a contribution of their own. Nowhere else, for example, is the real nature of his law practice—a mixture of important and inconsequential litigation in a variety of courts, both in Springfield and on the circuit—so graphically revealed. Nowhere else is the alternation of law and politics in his life so clearly shown. From no other treatise can one derive an understanding of the true character of the senatorial campaign of 1858, for the tendency of every writer has been to emphasize the seven formal debates and to ignore or minimize the daily speeches, the grinding travel, and the constant personal campaigning to which each candidate devoted all except a few days. Here, as faithfully as print can provide it, is a mirror-like replica of Lincoln's life.

In addition to the day-by-day record, each volume contains an introduction which the Lincoln student cannot afford to ignore. That in Pratt's first book is practically a biography of Lincoln for the first thirty years of his life, and is characterized by the author's mastery of detail, even in such matters as the exact cost of legislative banquets, the number of lawyers attending terms of the Supreme Court, and the number of roll calls in the legislature which Lincoln answered. Pratt's second introduction is shorter, and deals mainly with Lincoln's service in the legislature, his developing professional career, and his activities as a party manager and political candidate. Thomas's prefatory essay is mainly concerned with Lincoln's term in Congress and the law practice which he resumed with renewed determination after 1849. It is colorful as well as factual—a fine filling-out of the chronological framework. Angle, in the shortest of the four introductions, provides a compact summary of Lincoln's transition from a lawyer who had put politics behind him to a President appealing to his "dissatisfied fellow-countrymen" not to break up the Union.

The four books contain twelve maps depicting the Lincoln homes in Kentucky and Indiana, Lincoln's route in the Black Hawk War, the eighth circuit at various times, and Lincoln's travels and speeches in the major campaign years. Each volume has a full index.

Environmental Studies

IDA M. TARBELL.
    IN THE FOOTSTEPS OF THE LINCOLNS. 1924.

In this book Miss Tarbell, returning to the Lincoln theme twenty-three years after the publication of her biography, told the story of Lincoln and his forbears with particular reference to the places in which they lived. The book grew out of a pilgrimage which began at Hingham, where Samuel Lincoln settled in 1637, led through New Jersey, Pennsylvania, Virginia, Kentucky, and Indiana, and came to an end in Illinois. Throughout, the lives of Lincoln's ancestors are sketched against the background of environment. "I found it an inspiring thing," the author wrote in her preface, "to trace the roads these seven successive generations of Lincoln pioneers traveled, to look upon the remains of their homes, reconstruct from documents and legends their activities, judge what manner of men and women they were, the place they held among their fellows. In these wanderings the whole history of the United States seemed to unroll before me. In this Lincoln migration we have the family history of millions of our contemporaries."

In the Footsteps of the Lincolns, however, is more than an ancestral history. Approximately three-fourths of the book deals with Lincoln himself—in Kentucky and Indiana, in New Salem, in Springfield, and on the circuit. Although later research has proved some of Miss Tarbell's conclusions to be in error, the reader who wants an informal biography free from the hair-splittings of the specialists can still make no better choice.

Benjamin P. Thomas.
    LINCOLN'S NEW SALEM. 1934.

This is the story of a frontier town, of Lincoln's life there, and of the reconstruction of the village a century afterward. In writing it, the author was not content with tradition, as nearly all his predecessors had been. Instead, he searched court records and contemporary newspapers, and hunted out the letters of Lincoln's friends and neighbors in order to supplement and verify the old-age recollections of the villagers. As a result, his book has an authority that other studies lack.

This quality, however, was not achieved at the expense of interest, as is so often the case. *Lincoln's New Salem* is readable, even captivating—clear, straightforward, and sprinkled with humor. It is also marked by discernment. If there is a keener, more succinct appraisal of the effect of Lincoln's New Salem years on his growth and character than the paragraphs to be found on pages 89–90, this writer does not know where to find it.

Part Three, "New Salem Restored," is devoted to the legendary Lincoln of New Salem, and to the restoration of the village by the State of Illinois. Notwithstanding the fact that several structures, including the Rutledge mill, have been rebuilt since the book was written, the author's account of the restoration process has not been outmoded. There are notes, a map of New Salem, and drawings of the principal cabins.

THOMAS P. REEP.
   LINCOLN AT NEW SALEM. 1927.

Reep covered much the same ground as Thomas, but in a very different way. The latter's book is the finished product of a trained historian; Reep's is the work of a man born and bred in the New Salem neighborhood, and every page shows the mark of indigenous authorship. Reep is anecdotal, reminiscent, and homespun, and for these reasons conveys much of the authentic flavor of life in a village that passed out of existence more than a century ago. This is not to say, however, that the book is noticeably inaccurate, for its author, a lawyer, was well aware of the necessity of checking fallible memory against the existing records.

Reep has a long chapter, "Some of Lincoln's Friends and Associates at New Salem," which is a valuable collection of biographical sketches. The illustrations include charts of New Salem in Lincoln's day and facsimiles of documents in his handwriting.

PAUL M. ANGLE.
"HERE I HAVE LIVED": A HISTORY OF
LINCOLN'S SPRINGFIELD. 1935.

This book takes its title from two sentences in the short farewell address which Lincoln made to his friends and neighbors when he left Springfield forever on February 11, 1861. "To this place, and the kindness of these people, I owe everything. Here I have lived a quarter of a century, and have passed from a young to an old man." Obviously, words spoken under strong emotion should not be taken too literally, yet if there is any interaction between a man and his environment, these sentences have real meaning.

The author concluded that the best way to explain the nature and extent of Lincoln's confessed debt, if he actually had one, was to write the history of Springfield and place Lincoln in it with no more prominence than would have been accorded to him by a historian who was unaware of his posthumous fame. Therefore he started with the founding of the little prairie town and carried its story forward until May 4, 1865, when thousands gathered to lay Lincoln's body in a vault in Oak Ridge Cemetery. There are chapters in which Lincoln's name is not mentioned, and others—such as those which deal with politics in the 'forties, with the campaigns of the 'fifties, and with the election of 1860—in which he is the principal character. At the end, the reader must still draw his own conclusions as to Springfield's contribution to the making of a great man, but at least he has the material on which to base an opinion.

The book also has a secondary interest. The rise of the city has been a major phenomenon of American history since 1800, yet few historians have considered specific cities worthy of study. City histories, therefore, have been written, for the most part, by antiquarians, commercial hacks, or literary men bent on exploiting the quaint, the exotic, or the sinful. In this book, however, the author tried to write the history of a single city, and a small one at that, with the same detachment and the same regard for fact that he would have employed had the whole country been his subject. The book, therefore, is a document in American social history as well as a study of Lincoln's environment.

WILLIAM H. TOWNSEND.
  LINCOLN AND HIS WIFE'S
  HOME TOWN. 1929.

"It is the purpose of this book," Mr. Townsend asserted in his preface, "to show Lincoln's personal contacts with slavery which gave him a first-hand knowledge of the 'peculiar institution' that he could have acquired in no other way."

That purpose, Townsend decided, could be realized by telling the story of Lincoln's associations with Lexington, Kentucky, where Mrs. Lincoln was born and reared, and where members of her family continued to live after she removed to Springfield. Her father, Robert S. Todd, was a slave-holder, and in his home she, and later Lincoln, saw the more benevolent aspects of slavery. But the harsher side was never long out of sight. Slave auctions took place frequently, and revolting cruelties were matters of public knowledge. Thus, through his wife and through his own visits, Lincoln had opportunities infrequently accorded to Northerners for coming to a balanced conclusion about the most pressing question of his time.

But Townsend did more, in *Lincoln and His Wife's Home Town*, than prove this thesis. He provided, for the first time in Lincoln literature, a detailed and objective account of the Todds and their daughter Mary. He also sketched a gallery of distinguished Kentuckians of national prominence—Henry Clay, John J. Crittenden, John C. Breckinridge, the Confederate raider John Hunt Morgan, Robert J. Breckinridge, who did more than anyone else to hold Kentucky in the Union, and above all, Cassius M. Clay, abolitionist, soldier, diplomat, and eccentric.

Mr. Townsend's book, like Angle's "*Here I Have Lived*," is a case study in the history of American cities. In fulfilling his primary purpose the author naturally emphasized politics and slavery, but those subjects have broad ramifications. There is much to interest the student of social history, and the reader whose concern is with the Civil War will find three excellent chapters on Kentucky's role as a Border State.

NOAH BROOKS.
WASHINGTON IN LINCOLN'S TIME. 1895.

The reader who wants the kind of environmental study that Townsend made of Lexington will not find it here.[2] This, rather, is a book of reminiscences, but one which throws much light on the Washington of Lincoln's presidency. It covers a wide range of subjects. There are sketches of leading members of Congress and important government officials. There are accounts of Lincoln's visit to the Army of the Potomac soon after Hooker was put at its head, of social events at the White House, of Lincoln's appearances at the theater. Washington's dismay at the news of Fredericksburg and Chancellorsville, its fears at the time of Early's raid, its joy after Gettysburg, its jubilation and relief when Lee surrendered, are described. The President's attitude towards the convention that nominated him in 1864, his reception of the returns of the election of that year, and his second inauguration are the subjects of interesting sections. The aftermath of the assassination and the trial of the conspirators are not neglected. The book ends with a stirring account of the grand review of the Army of the Potomac and the Army of the West.

Noah Brooks was well qualified to write of Lincoln and the city of Washington. Before the war, as a resident of Dixon, Illinois, he came to know the future President as a Republican leader. After 1862 he was in Washington as the correspondent of the *Sacramento Union*. Lincoln liked and

[2]For that, Margaret Leech's *Reveille in Washington* is recommended. Her book is not given extended notice here because Lincoln appears only incidentally.

trusted him to such an extent that he was planning to make him his private secretary at the time of his own death.

Professional Career

A. A. WOLDMAN.
   LAWYER LINCOLN. 1936.

Abraham Lincoln practiced law from 1837 to 1860, and from 1861 to 1865 he was face to face with national problems which were largely legal in character. Yet only a few books deal exclusively with this phase of his life, and only one—this work—is a comprehensive study.

Earlier writers—notably Frederick Trevor Hill (*Lincoln the Lawyer*) and John T. Richards (*Lincoln the Lawyer-Statesman*)—limited themselves to accounts of Lincoln's professional preparation, his partnerships, a small number of typical cases, and major constitutional problems. Mr. Woldman covers these matters and much more besides— the members of the bar with whom Lincoln was most closely associated, on the circuit as well as in Springfield; the unimportant cases to which much of his time was necessarily devoted; his services as a *de facto* judge and states attorney; the fees he charged and the investments he made; the law suits in which he was involved as principal. His closing chapters deal with the Dred Scott decision, Lincoln's legal duel with Chief Justice Taney, and the major constitutional questions occasioned by the Civil War.

This is a thorough book, and one which is based on a careful combing of a wide range of printed sources. However, it lacks the sure touch which familiarity with the unprinted sources—dust-covered files, records, and dockets in a dozen courthouses—would have given its author. But this is a minor defect even to specialists, and no defect at all to the great majority of readers.

HENRY C. WHITNEY.
LIFE ON THE CIRCUIT WITH LINCOLN. 1892.

This is the classic account of the carefree, nomadic practice of the law in which Lincoln was engaged for almost half of every year. The author was a young lawyer when he first met Lincoln at Urbana, Illinois, in 1854; thereafter, in spite of the difference in their ages, the two men were on friendly terms. Whitney tried cases with Lincoln, watched him try others, listened to him on the stump, and took part in the arguing and story-telling and horse-play by which judge, lawyers, and litigants amused themselves in the comfortless country inns. Then, years afterward, he wrote colorfully of what he remembered.

Unfortunately, he wrote of more than what he remembered. Whitney was nothing if not discursive, so the reader finds discourses on Napoleon, Washington, Julius Caesar, John the Baptist, and Socrates; essays on the military genius of a line of commanders from Alexander the Great to Von Moltke; a history of Cincinnati; and other matters as far removed from Lincoln and the eighth judicial circuit as one pole from the other. He also finds one example of Whitney's creative ability—a "newly discovered" speech which by the author's statement Lincoln delivered at Urbana in the fall of 1854, but which turns out to be the famous Peoria speech of that same year, thinly disguised.

Notwithstanding his delinquencies—and they were real ones[3]—Whitney's book deserves the popularity it has long enjoyed. Except for the one major aberration that has been noted it is surprisingly accurate, and its portrayal of a lawyer's life ninety years ago remains unsurpassed.

Political Career

EDWIN ERLE SPARKS.
THE LINCOLN-DOUGLAS DEBATES OF 1858. 1908.

The editor of this volume—the only source in which one can find the text of the Lincoln-Douglas debates as they were officially reported—described the features that justify its inclusion here:

Many editions of the debates have been printed, beginning with that of 1860; a few have included speeches made by each participant, both before and after the set debates; some have added explanatory footnotes; but none have attempted to reproduce the local color from the press of the day. In this edition an effort is made by newspaper extracts and by reminiscences to give a picture of the crude though virile setting in this contest of two men so evenly matched in polemical power, yet so unlike in temperament and physical appearance. Only those seven speeches are here reprinted which were delivered at the seven set meetings constituting in reality the Great Debate. The gist of the prior speeches is woven into the introduction.

The newspaper excerpts, culled from files in dozens of libraries, convey the flavor of the time with a degree of fidelity which no secondary account can achieve. Here are

[3] These delinquencies are discussed at some length in the introduction to my edition of *Life on the Circuit*, published by The Caxton Printers, 1940. Here also is to be found a critique of Whitney's version of Lincoln's "Lost Speech" at Bloomington, May 29, 1856.

the dusty streets of small Illinois towns, the bands and floats, partisans and hecklers, Black Republicans, Squatter Sovereigns, and Danites—all the trappings of politics as Lincoln knew it. For the real "feel" of the past, this book is invaluable.

WILLIAM E. BARINGER.
LINCOLN'S RISE TO POWER. 1937.

On the 16th of June, 1858, Abraham Lincoln was nominated as the Republican candidate for United States Senator from Illinois. He responded by delivering what came to be known as his "House Divided" speech. Partly because of that speech, he was defeated by Stephen A. Douglas. Yet in less than two years from the day of its delivery he was nominated for the presidency, with election certain to follow.

The story of this amazing advancement—the "rise to power"—is Baringer's theme. Of course it was told many times before the appearance of his book, but never with this abundance of detail. Contemporary newspapers furnished the author with much of the material and most of the flavor; the papers of Salmon P. Chase, Lyman Trumbull, John McLean, Elihu B. Washburne, and others revealed what was going on behind the scenes; and dozens of memoirs and special studies rounded out the record. —Which is to say that the book rests on a firm documentary foundation.

Baringer shows that Lincoln did not become a serious contender for the nomination until three or four months before the national convention. He also makes clear the fact that Lincoln was his own campaign manager—that he guided the movement that resulted in his nomination, and in the process gave proof of the acumen that was later to be recognized as one of his outstanding characteristics. The convention itself is the subject of several chapters in which the author's flair for vivid narrative is evident. A few pages are devoted to the campaign which resulted in Lincoln's election, but the book really ends with the nomination.

Occasional strainings for literary effect and too-long-sustained sprightliness are minor blemishes in an able piece of research and writing.

REINHARD H. LUTHIN.
THE FIRST LINCOLN CAMPAIGN. 1944.

Where Baringer told a story, Luthin analyzes. First comes an account of the origin and growth of the Republican party, with a summary of the interests—tariffs, internal improvements, homesteads, national expansion—that attracted thousands of voters who were not greatly concerned about slavery. A parade of the pre-convention candidates follows. Separate chapters are devoted to the political careers of Seward, Chase, Bates, Cameron, and Lincoln; such minor aspirants as Nathaniel P. Banks, John McLean, Ben Wade, and Cassius M. Clay receive much shorter notices. After an account of the break-up of the Democratic party come the familiar story of Lincoln's nomination—Luthin strikes it off as "the triumph of availability"—a narrative of the progress of the campaign, and an analysis of the factors that contributed to Republican victory.

The First Lincoln Campaign covers familiar ground, but it has its own claims to distinction: more emphasis than usual on the importance of economic factors, and much more documentation. The citations—1527 notes for 225 pages— refer to a wide range of manuscripts and newspaper files, and to every printed source of consequence.

WILLIAM E. BARINGER.
A HOUSE DIVIDING. 1945.

The subtitle of this book, "Lincoln as President Elect," indicates that it is a study of the four months from November 6, 1860, to March 4, 1861, and therefore a sequel to the author's *Lincoln's Rise to Power*.

Here Baringer stresses two themes: Lincoln's selection of his cabinet, and his attitude towards secession. The first theme is treated with so much detail that the machinations of politicians and the speculations of newspaper correspondents become something of a strain on the reader's patience. Baringer possesses real narrative skill, but too often, in this book, he abdicates in favor of correspondents and editorial writers. Nevertheless, these same quotations will be welcomed by close students of the period.

Baringer's handling of his second theme—Lincoln's attitude towards secession—and his account of the trip from Springfield to Washington for the inauguration are of secondary importance.

DAVID M. POTTER.
LINCOLN AND HIS PARTY IN THE SECESSION CRISIS. 1942.

Potter's subject is the attitude of Lincoln and Seward, and to a lesser extent, other Republican leaders, towards secession from the time of the presidential election in 1860 to the attack on Fort Sumter. His book is analysis and argument rather than narrative. During this critical period Lincoln purposely kept in the background and concealed his thoughts and intentions so effectively that historians have contented themselves with recitals of his activities and summaries of his public utterances. Potter's task, therefore, was to scrutinize the available material, compare the sources, and deduce Lincoln's intentions. So well did he perform it that his book will stand as the definitive treatment unless some now unknown body of source material makes major corrections necessary.

Potter has gone far beyond Lincoln's determination to maintain the Union. How was it to be maintained? he asks. "Could he [Lincoln] save it without compromise? Could he save it without war? Could he save it by a purely negative policy, and, if not, what positive measures were required?"

The answers to these questions are too involved, the argument too close-knit, to be summarized. However, it may not be misleading to say that the author contends— proves even—that at the time of his inauguration, Lincoln not only expected the Union to be saved, but believed that it could be saved without war. But the Sumter crisis forced his hand. He was willing to see Fort Sumter go if Fort Pickens could be held and made to serve as the symbol of national authority, but the Pickens expedition was bungled so badly that Anderson's provisions gave out first. As Lincoln saw it, he had no alternative to ordering relief to Sumter. Then war came.

Potter's book ends with a Bibliographical Note which

is an illuminating description of his methods as well as a valuable commentary on sources.

T. HARRY WILLIAMS.
   LINCOLN AND THE RADICALS. 1941.

Lincoln and the Radicals is the story of the four-year struggle, no holds barred, between Lincoln and the extremists of his own party. It is not a pretty story. Ben Wade, Zachariah Chandler, Thad Stevens, and their followers in the House and Senate; Chase and Stanton in the cabinet; McDowell, Fremont, Pope, Burnside, Hooker, Butler, and many a lesser officer in the army are shown playing politics—and often pretty sordid politics—for all the game was worth.

Williams contends that the Radicals won. This view overlooks the fact that emancipation, as Lincoln proclaimed it, was far short of what they wanted; that the confiscation acts were less severe than would have been the case had they had their way; and that reconstruction was a drawn battle while Lincoln lived. The reader should also be reminded that politics, even in the eye-gouging form which the Radicals adopted, was only a phase of the Civil War. In the summer of 1864, for example, when they were certain that Lincoln would withdraw from the presidential contest in favor of a more extreme candidate, Sherman's sixty thousand veterans were slashing into the heart of the Confederacy. They, and not a handful of zealots in Congress, were shaping events.

These comments are not intended to invalidate Williams' study, but only to suggest that some of his conclusions and implications be scrutinized. The book rests on a thorough familiarity with the sources, it is carefully documented, and every page offers evidence that it is the work of a scholar who can write.

HARRY J. CARMAN AND REINHARD H. LUTHIN.
  LINCOLN AND THE PATRONAGE. 1943.

That Lincoln was one of the most astute politicians who ever held the presidential office is a truism. Nevertheless, until recently most of those who accepted the validity of the characterization would have been hard put to prove it. They could have cited the skill with which he placated his rivals, balanced section against section and Democrat against Old Whig in the formation of his cabinet; they could have adduced to their support his handling of the Border States in the first months of the war; they could have drawn evidence from his course with reference to emancipation. But such matters as these are not politics as the man in the street understands it.

To Carman and Luthin, as to most men, politics means jobs. What part did Lincoln have in ousting the Democrats from Federal offices, and how did he fill their places? In answering these questions, the authors describe the selecting of cabinet officers and foreign ministers, but collectorships, postmasters, marshals, and army officers are by no means beneath their dignity. Neither are contracts and commissions. When E. A. Allen informed Thurlow Weed that he had 42,000 rifles and muskets which he wanted to sell to the government, and promised to compensate the New Yorker *"fully"* for his help, he probably never suspected that his letter would appear in print eighty-one years later, but here it is. Here also are dozens of other proposals equally brazen, and accounts of hundreds of transactions and appointments on a plane not much higher.

Lincoln and the Patronage is almost an encyclopedia of the more prominent members of the Republican party, and many of its lesser lights, from 1860 to 1865. The thoroughness of the authors, and their success in turning up the details of many a transaction which the principals must have hoped was forgotten, will command the admiration of everyone who has ever attempted historical research. Their bibliography lists fifty-nine collections of manuscripts in twenty-one repositories, forty-five newspaper files, and five hundred printed sources. From such patient work lasting books are made.

TYLER DENNETT.
LINCOLN AND THE CIVIL WAR. 1939.

From 1861 until 1868 John Hay kept a diary. During the same period, and afterward, he wrote some of the freest, most colorful letters that have ever come from the pen of an American. The diary, supplemented by letters, makes up this book.

As readers of Nicolay and Hay's life of Lincoln know, Hay drew freely from his diary for that work. After his death, Mrs. Hay made selections from the diary and Hay's letters, had them printed in three volumes, and distributed approximately 200 copies to friends. Proper names, however, were represented only by initial letters. This device, and the small number of copies, limited the book's usefulness. There was a real place, therefore, for Tyler Dennett's edition of the diary and letters. *Lincoln and the Civil War* is larger than the privately printed selection, all names are given in full, and there are suitable annotations and satisfactory indexes.

In spite of several long gaps, Hay's diary and letters are an important Lincoln source. As Dennett well says: "They may be read for information, for remarkable vignettes of remarkable people, for a sense of the social and political atmosphere of war-time Washington . . . or they may be read merely for amusement." Whatever the reader's motive, the result will be an unforgettable picture of a very great man.

Commander-in-Chief

COLIN R. BALLARD.
   THE MILITARY GENIUS OF ABRAHAM
   LINCOLN. 1926.

Before the publication of this essay the predominant opinion of Lincoln as a military leader was critical.[4] Most military historians took the position that he was too prone to interfere with the professional soldiers who commanded the armies in the field. The general and special war orders which he issued early in 1862, his detention of McDowell's Corps during the Peninsular Campaign, and his sharply critical attitude towards Meade after the Battle of Gettysburg have been favorite examples.

[4]Ballard's book was not the only factor in effecting a revision. Credit must also be given to *Washington, Lincoln, Wilson: Three War Statesmen* and other writings of John M. Palmer, and to Sir Frederick Maurice's *Statesmen and Soldiers of the Civil War*. Ballard's work is given preference here because it is concerned more directly with Lincoln than the other writings cited.

General Ballard, an English soldier, finds that in these and other instances of "interference" Lincoln was not without justification. His case for the War President's military genius, however, rests on broader grounds. Lincoln, he contends, was the forerunner of what we know today as the High Command.[5] In that capacity he recognized immediately the North's superior naval power and made the most of it. He was aware of the interdependence of strategic and political considerations. He constantly urged that pressure be maintained all along the line—that the Confederate armies be assailed in the western theater and along the southeastern seaboard as well as in Virginia. He saw, more clearly than most of his generals, that the main body of the enemy, not enemy territory, was the true objective. And he insisted that there be no half-measures—that the Union could be restored only when Southern military power was destroyed.

In *The Military Genius of Abraham Lincoln* General Ballard sticks closely to his subject, and goes into the history of actual military operations no more fully than is necessary for an understanding of Lincoln's role as commander-in-chief.

Constitutional Problems

JAMES G. RANDALL.
  CONSTITUTIONAL PROBLEMS UNDER
  LINCOLN. 1926.

To understand just what this book is, one should emphasize the least prominent word in the title. Professor Randall,

---

[5] In World War II, the American and British heads of state and the Joint Chiefs of Staff.

with the reverence for absolute accuracy that characterizes all his work, did well to call it *Constitutional Problems Under Lincoln* instead of *Lincoln and the Constitutional Problems of His Administration*, or *Lincoln and the Constitution During the Civil War*, as a less scrupulous scholar might have done.

For Lincoln, in these pages, plays a subordinate role. The subject, rather, is the constitutional problems which beset the government between 1861 and 1865. Those problems were far more numerous and far more complex than is generally realized. One may name the war powers of the President and Congress, the question of belligerency as it concerned the Confederacy, the status of the Confederate leaders with reference to the law of treason, habeas corpus, arbitrary arrests, martial law, conscription, emancipation, and the partition of Virginia without completing a mere listing. Naturally, Lincoln's attitude towards all these subjects is indicated, but Randall is concerned with the acts and opinions of cabinet officers, judges, and the military much more often than with those of the President.

Randall's approach is not that of the legalist. "Constitutional history," he asserts, "is not the study of a document, but rather of a social process—the process by which a community re-expresses from time to time its will concerning its government, refitting, reinterpreting and expanding its fundamental law so as to keep abreast of new ideas." This point of view enables him to point out that while Lincoln used more arbitrary power than any other President has assumed—the reader will note the date of publication—he used it in such a way that American liberties were not permanently impaired. "His humane sympathy, his humor, his lawyerlike caution, his common sense, his fairness toward opponents, his dislike of arbitrary rule, his willingness to take the people into his confidence and to set forth patiently the reasons for unusual measures" —these characteristics, Randall finds, led him to be criticized "for leniency as often as for severity."

In a democracy, war raises or intensifies many fundamental problems of government. Published eight years after the end of the first World War, *Constitutional Problems Under Lincoln* is an implicit commentary—and in places an explicit one—on the course of Wilson's administration. A second World War has again made it timely.

Foreign Affairs

Jay Monaghan.
DIPLOMAT IN CARPET SLIPPERS. 1945.

Lincoln's handling of foreign affairs is a subject which almost every biographer has touched upon. Few, however, have dealt with more than the sharpest international crises produced by the Civil War. To this statement the work of Nicolay and Hay is the most notable exception, but even in that book there is not to be found anything like Monaghan's fullness of detail.

Completeness, therefore, is the first virtue of *Diplomat in Carpet Slippers*. The well known episodes—the seizure of Mason and Slidell, the Laird rams, Napoleon's Mexican venture, for example—are treated at length, as one would expect; but there are also accounts of incidents and problems unknown except by close students of diplomatic history. The proffer of a command to Garibaldi, the activities of Northern and Southern propagandists in Europe, Confederate plans to abolish slavery in return for recognition by France and Great Britain—this is only a random sampling of subjects which the reader will find in few if any of the standard Lincoln biographies.

The book's second virtue is liveliness. Monaghan writes history at a playwright's pace and with a playwright's flair for drama. The *dramatis personae*, moreover, are given their full due. In fact, *Diplomat in Carpet Slippers* derives no small part of its interest from the personalities of those who figure in its pages. William H. Seward, Lincoln's secretary of state; Charles Sumner, the Senator most influential in foreign affairs; Cassius M. Clay, the Kentucky swashbuckler whom Lincoln sent to Russia; Adam Gurowski, the caustic, eccentric Pole whose diary is a principal though unreliable source of war-time history; John Bright, Palmerston, and Lord John Russell among the British; Napoleon III of France; John Slidell and James Mason for the Confederates—these and many others cease to be names from the somnolent past and join the circle of the reader's acquaintances.

But the drama and high readability of *Diplomat in Carpet Slippers* are slightly misleading. In Monaghan's pages Seward is likely to "scream" or "screech" when the evidence indicates only that he was under tension; Thurlow Weed is always the wily wire-puller; to Lincoln himself is often imputed cognizance, even guidance, of international manipulations without clear evidential warrant—which is to say that there are times when Monaghan allows his

flair for drama to tip the scales against the strict require-
ments of history. Fortunately, such lapses are neither frequent enough nor important enough to be serious.

The Gettysburg Address

WILLIAM E. BARTON.
   LINCOLN AT GETTYSBURG. 1930.

Lincoln's Gettysburg Address offers a striking example of
the difficulties that beset the historian. Dozens, perhaps
hundreds, of books and articles deal with phases of the subject—the writing of the address, the sources which Lincoln
drew upon, the actual delivery, the reaction of the audience, the manner in which the speech was received by the
country as a whole. Many of the authors had first-hand
knowledge and no desire but to record the truth, yet
their accounts are hopelessly at variance. One can cite
evidence that Lincoln wrote the address in Washington
and that he made no preparation at all, that he read
from a manuscript and that he spoke without manuscript, that the audience cheered and remained silent
as he closed.

From this mass of contradictory testimony, Dr. Barton
set out to establish what actually happened. By reviewing
the evidence, comparing statements, and subjecting the
testimony to the test of common sense, he established these
essential facts beyond reasonable doubt: that Lincoln wrote
the address before he left Washington, that he spoke it from
memory with only an occasional glance at the manuscript,
that there was only perfunctory applause when he finished,

and that the newspapers of the time paid little attention to what he said. Barton also described the genesis of the national cemetery, analyzed the sources of the address, included a long chapter of excerpts from the recollections of men who were in Lincoln's audience, and printed Edward Everett's oration in full.

The book suffers, in minor degree, from the discursiveness that characterizes so much of Dr. Barton's writing, and from the speculative propensity that led him to include a chapter on what Lincoln wished he had said. Nevertheless, it is not likely that anything of consequence will be added to his findings or conclusions.

Reconstruction

CHARLES H. MCCARTHY.
  LINCOLN'S PLAN OF RECONSTRUCTION.
  1901.

This book covers much more ground than its title indicates. Lincoln's plan of reconstruction, to be sure, is described in detail, as is also the divergent plan matured by the Radical Republicans. In addition, the author traces the course of political events—secession, the restoration of national authority, reconstruction—in Tennessee, Louisiana, Arkansas, and Virginia (including the separation of West Virginia); anti-slavery proclamations and legislation; and the abortive attempts of Horace Greeley, Francis P. Blair, and James R. Gilmore to make peace between the warring sections.

Few books are better examples than this of Freeman's

dictum that the essence of history is past politics.[6] Of social, economic, and even political conditions in the states of the South there is only the barest mention. Instead, the narrative centers in Washington, and especially in the Capitol and the White House. Necessarily, the contest between Lincoln and the Radicals of his own party plays a prominent part. In this respect, *Lincoln's Plan of Reconstruction* is in curious contrast with Williams' *Lincoln and the Radicals*.[7] The two books cover the same general ground yet the points of view and methods of their authors are so far apart that neither makes the other dispensable. For personalities, drama, motives, and the historian's appraisal of them, see Williams; for all the aspects of reconstruction as they came to one great issue in Washington, McCarthy's study continues to be an essential book.

Reminiscences

EMANUEL HERTZ.
THE HIDDEN LINCOLN. 1938.

In this volume are printed the most important of the source materials on which Herndon's biography of Lincoln was based. Included are more than 150 letters from Herndon to such men as Charles Henry Hart, Ward Hill Lamon, Truman H. Bartlett, and Jesse W. Weik; letters to Herndon from Horace White, Dennis Hanks, Joseph Gillespie, Leonard Swett, R. B. Rutledge, and others who knew Lincoln well; statements by John Hanks, Mrs. Ninian W. Edwards,

---

[6]"Between history and politics I can draw no distinction. History is the politics of the past; politics are the history of the present."

[7]See pp. 86–87.

Henry C. Whitney, and others in position to know much of Lincoln's story; and a number of Herndon's own notes and memoranda.

For making these documents generally available Mr. Hertz deserves the gratitude of all students of Lincoln's life. His editorial deficiencies, however, cannot be overlooked. There are mistakes in the transcribing of proper names— "Sherman's defeat," for example, in place of Stillman's defeat—which would not have been made by an editor thoroughly versed in Lincoln's life. More important is Hertz's neglect to place his presumably superior knowledge at the reader's disposal. Thus Herndon's statements that Thomas Lincoln left Kentucky because of his wife's infidelity, that Lincoln's mother was illegitimate, and that Lincoln himself was the son of unmarried parents—and these are only examples—stand without correction or qualification. In the entire text, which occupies more than 400 pages, there are only twenty-one footnotes, of which not one is either critical or interpretative. In a book in which almost every page cries for interpretation, such restraint is equivalent to abdication of the editorial function. A compilation that could have been enormously valuable to the general reading public is actually often misleading except to the relatively small number of students who are themselves capable of correcting its many errors. Only for the Introduction—a well-deserved tribute to Herndon and his biographical labors—can Hertz's editing be commended without reservations.

Isaac N. Phillips.
    ABRAHAM LINCOLN, BY SOME MEN WHO
    KNEW HIM. 1910.

Though small in size and unpretentious in title, this book makes an immediate claim to the reader's confidence. None of the five contributors professed to have been an intimate of Lincoln, and each was content to write of what he knew at first hand. All were younger by twenty or twenty-five years than their subject, and all claimed only that they knew him as young men of one generation know a man of the next earlier one. Their recollections, nevertheless, constitute a composite character sketch that has consistency, reality, and vividness.

The strongest impression conveyed by these reminiscences is of Lincoln's natural dignity. "To portray Lincoln as ill-mannered, uncouth, unrefined in sentiment, the indulger of vulgarity of speech, a buffoon and yarn-spinner," wrote Owen T. Reeves, who practiced law with him for several years, "is a complete and outrageous caricature." "No one called Mr. Lincoln 'Abe,'" James S. Ewing asserted. Equally positive is John W. Bunn's statement: "I never heard any man call Mr. Lincoln 'Abe' in his own presence." These men and the other two contributors— Richard Price Morgan and Franklin Blades—wrote of Lincoln's humor, his frank and cordial manner towards his associates, and his political acumen, but they emphasized repeatedly that vulgarity and clownishness were foreign to his nature, and that reserve and dignity were deep-grained traits.

Mr. Phillips dedicated this modest compilation "to those

who have read volumes of Lincoln biographies in a vain effort to form a correct estimate of Lincoln, the man." Most readers will agree that it serves the purpose implied in the dedication.

ALLEN THORNDIKE RICE.
REMINISCENCES OF ABRAHAM LINCOLN BY DISTINGUISHED MEN OF HIS TIME. 1886.

The title of this book suggests a melancholy question: How many men distinguished in Lincoln's time are still familiar figures? Put specifically, how many well informed readers today can identify Leonard Swett, Elihu B. Washburne, Lawrence Weldon, Charles Carleton Coffin, George W. Julian, E. W. Andrews, Ben Perley Poore, or Donn Piatt? The answer, of course, is few. But the answer is unimportant, for, remembered or not, these men contributed reminiscences of value to Rice's compilation. Swett and Weldon, lawyers of Bloomington, Illinois, wrote informatively and engagingly of Lincoln's youth and of his career at the Illinois bar; Washburne described his rise from political obscurity to the leadership of the Republican party; the other contributors named above related many interesting incidents which happened between 1860 and 1865.

Rice included the recollections of a number of men whose fame has lasted—Ben Butler, Henry Ward Beecher, Walt Whitman, and Robert G. Ingersoll. Whitman's contribution is interesting but brief; Butler's, though not entirely reliable, is of value; Beecher wrote just what one would expect; and Ingersoll is represented by the concluding section of his famous Lincoln oration.

In a revised edition, published in 1909, twelve reminiscences which appeared in the original publication were omitted. Several—notably those by W. D. Kelley, Schuyler Colfax, James B. Fry, David R. Locke, and Thomas Hicks —are at least as interesting as those which were retained.

This collection suffers from the same editorial deficiencies that characterize *The Hidden Lincoln*. Many names are misspelled, and there is no annotation.

Francis B. Carpenter.
SIX MONTHS AT THE WHITE HOUSE WITH ABRAHAM LINCOLN. 1866.

Near the end of 1863 Carpenter, a young artist, conceived the idea of painting a picture to commemorate the issuance of the Proclamation of Emancipation. Through the intercession of influential friends he gained the consent of Lincoln; his own likeable qualities won the President's confidence and cooperation. For several months in 1864 he had the run of the White House, an almost unparalleled opportunity to observe Lincoln, and many chances for free conversation.

Day after day he watched the people throng into Lincoln's office with their stories of injustice and suffering. He heard Lincoln's own account of his decision to abolish slavery by proclamation; heard him recite, and criticize, passages from "Hamlet" and "Richard III"; heard him read his favorite poem, "Mortality," and Oliver Wendell Holmes's "The Last Leaf." From cabinet members and other prominent men he got many sidelights and anecdotes. To these he added his own impressions and observations, and excerpts from recently published reminiscences by such men as W. D. Kelley, J. P. Gulliver, and William H. Herndon.

Carpenter's transparent sincerity, his general accuracy, and not-negligible literary skill combined to make his book immediately and lastingly popular.

Issues published in 1868 and later are entitled *The Inner Life of Abraham Lincoln.*

ALEXANDER K. McCLURE.
ABRAHAM LINCOLN AND MEN OF
WAR-TIMES. 1892.

This is an uncommonly instructive book of wartime reminiscences. The author, a prominent Pennsylvania Republican, had many opportunities to talk with Lincoln and leaders of his administration, and to know what was going on beneath the surface from 1861 to 1865. Endowed with a trained mind and tenacious memory, he was able, in his recollections, to throw considerable light on events and personalities that were not always quite what they seemed. His appraisal of Cameron, for example, is much more convincing than the all-black characterization that passes current; his analysis of Lincoln as a politician is unsurpassed; his account of Lincoln's part in the nomination of Andrew Johnson, though vigorously challenged, is testimony of fundamental importance.

Abraham Lincoln and Men of War-Times starts with an account of the Republican National Convention of 1860. Then follow several chapters in which Lincoln, whom the author first met in January, 1861, is the central figure.

These give way to accounts of Lincoln's relations with the leading men of his day—Chase, Cameron, Stanton, Grant, McClellan, Sherman, Greeley, and others. Chapters on Lincoln and Andrew G. Curtin, Pennsylvania's great war governor, Lincoln and Thad Stevens, and Lincoln and Buchanan contain judgments which, though unorthodox, certainly deserve consideration. The book concludes with McClure's recollections of wartime experiences in the Cumberland Valley of Pennsylvania and with an account of the services of the Pennsylvania Reserve Corps. An acrimonious exchange of correspondence between McClure and John G. Nicolay over the nomination of Johnson in 1864 constitutes an Appendix.

Rufus Rockwell Wilson.
LINCOLN AMONG HIS FRIENDS. 1942.

In this volume Mr. Wilson has assembled fifty-three reminiscences of Lincoln, all from printed sources, and has arranged them in general chronological order. Each is preceded by a brief note identifying the author and the place of original publication.

A critical reader is more likely to be impressed by the book's deficiencies than by its good qualities. Many of the reminiscences deal with trivial matters; many—notably those which appeared originally in the *Century*—are well known; several come through the medium of reporters whose accuracy cannot be evaluated; and most were written many years after the events with which they are concerned. Nevertheless, it is a convenience to have even these in one readily accessible volume.

Besides, there are a number of really valuable contributions. The recollections of Lincoln as a lawyer by James C. Conkling, James O. Cunningham, Lambert Tree, Charles S. Zane, and Abram Bergen have genuine substance. "A Sculptor's Recollections of Lincoln," by Thomas D. Jones, deserves many readers. The accounts of Lincoln's assassination by Lawrence A. Gobright, Mrs. William A. Brown, and Dr. Charles S. Taft are vivid pieces of reporting. Noah Brooks's "Impressions," written and published soon after Lincoln's death; Horace Greeley's estimate of Lincoln, written about 1870 though not published until 1891; and the long book review, by Albert T. Bledsoe, which Mr. Wilson calls a "wrong-headed but in many ways illuminating survey," have continuing interest.

RUFUS ROCKWELL WILSON.
INTIMATE MEMORIES OF LINCOLN. 1945.

Mr. Wilson's second collection of reminiscences is a decided advance over *Lincoln Among His Friends*. There are eighty-odd contributions instead of fifty-three, and in spite of the inclusion of such old favorites as John Hay's account of life in the White House and A. K. McClure's story of Lincoln's part in Johnson's nomination for the vice-presidency, they come from more obscure sources. Many, moreover, were recorded at earlier dates than those in the first collection. As in the other book, the arrangement is chronological, and each contribution is preceded by a prefatory note in which the author is identified and the place of first publication indicated.

At least two pieces which Mr. Wilson included stand out

as items of first importance. One is a long letter, written only ten days after the event, in which Leonard Swett related the inside story of Lincoln's nomination for the presidency in 1860. The other is a hitherto unpublished account, by Gideon Welles, of Lincoln's selection of his cabinet.

Like most collections of reminiscences, this one is marked by unevenness, inconsistency, error, and repetition. Its value would have been greater had the editor corrected, qualified, or amplified more of the assertions of his contributors—in other words, had his annotations been more numerous and thorough—but that seems to be a labor which those who compile books of this kind are unwilling to undertake.

The Personality of Lincoln

Jesse W. Weik.
    THE REAL LINCOLN: A PORTRAIT. 1922.

According to the author's Foreword, this book owes its inception to Leonard Swett. Visiting him in Chicago soon after the publication of Herndon's *Lincoln*, Weik found that while Swett spoke favorably of that book, he believed it was not what it might have been. Swett, as Weik reported the conversation, held that Herndon "had failed to bring out as fully as he should the human side of Lincoln, the incidents of his domestic and home life, and especially a definite and searching insight into his activities as a lawyer . . . ; that not enough attention had been given to Mr. Lincoln's Springfield environment . . . ; that there should be more local color, more of the details of his personal history as revealed by his neighbors—in short, the doors of his office and of his home should be made to swing open and the light turned on so that we may indeed view him as a man." Weik decided to act on Swett's suggestion, although more than thirty years were to elapse before the book embodying it appeared.

The Real Lincoln is an amplification of the more personal parts of Herndon's *Lincoln*. Lincoln's courtship and marriage, his domestic life, his relations with women, his interests and amusements, his propensity to put too much confidence in unworthy friends—these, plus much material about his practice of law—are Weik's principal topics. To develop them he drew heavily upon the Herndon manuscripts in his possession, but he also quoted freely from such old friends of Lincoln as Swett, Whitney, David Davis, and John W. Bunn. His own research in court records and contemporary newspapers yielded some matters of interest.

Weik's attitude on the controversial subjects of Lincoln's life—his ancestry, his marriage, the personality of Mrs. Lincoln—are identical with Herndon's. Informal, interesting, filled with welcome though often unimportant detail, his book can best be described as a long footnote to the great biography of which he was co-author.

JOSEPH FORT NEWTON.
    LINCOLN AND HERNDON. 1910.

For five critical years—from 1854 to 1859—William H. Herndon carried on a correspondence with Theodore Parker. Half a century later these letters, as yet unpublished, were made available to Joseph Fort Newton, then a young clergyman in Cedar Rapids, Iowa. Out of them

Newton fashioned a book which for originality, historical importance, and literary charm is still one of a select few among Lincoln studies.

Herndon, characteristically, wrote often, at length, and with enthusiasm. (Fifty-two letters to Parker are printed in full.) His principal subjects, aside from philosophical speculation, were the rise of the anti-slavery movement in Illinois, the growth of the Republican party, and, as he came into prominence, Abraham Lincoln. Herndon's political comments throw valuable light on the point of view of the more radical element of the party, while what he wrote of Lincoln, though long since merged in the stream of biography, remains a contemporary portrait of unsurpassed fidelity. Parker's letters, fewer in number and less effusive, served principally to keep the correspondence alive.

Into the Herndon-Parker letters Dr. Newton, with rare skill, fitted a study of Herndon, Lincoln, and the relations between them. The book is not a biography, but in it are to be found more of the facts of Herndon's life than are to be found elsewhere, and also the fullest portrayal of his personality. Lincoln's career is traced in detail through the period covered by the correspondence. The book ends with a sympathetic, yet generally sound, appraisal of the Herndon biography.

HELEN NICOLAY.
   PERSONAL TRAITS OF ABRAHAM
   LINCOLN. 1912.

In the Preface to this little book Miss Nicolay relates that when her father began collecting material for the biography which he and John Hay were to write he put certain memoranda into an envelope marked "Personal Traits" with the intention of including a chapter under that heading. As the work grew, the one envelope expanded into many, but at the same time Nicolay slowly came to the conclusion that a chapter on this subject would be out of place in a long and formal biography. Instead, he decided to use what he had gathered in a smaller, more intimate volume of his own authorship. For one reason or another, the book never appeared.

Miss Nicolay would have the reader believe that these unused notes of her father form the materials out of which *Personal Traits of Abraham Lincoln* was put together. It is no disparagement to say that this is only partly true. To be sure, she has made good use of her father's memoranda, sometimes openly crediting an anecdote or a personal letter to him, sometimes attributing a characteristic revelation to "a member of the President's household," and sometimes veiling her source so fully that only those who are completely at home in Lincoln literature can recognize it. Just as often she has made her own blending of material drawn from sources other than her father's notes—reminiscences of Lincoln's contemporaries, and the President's own writings and sayings. And none needs be sorry that this is the case, for her own contributions are no less appealing, no less illustrative of Lincoln's personality, than those of her father.

Personal Traits of Abraham Lincoln is just what its title implies. Chapters deal with Lincoln's anecdotes, with the life he led on the circuit, with his attitude towards money, with life in the White House, with his relations with his wife and children, his secretariat and the cabinet, with his kindness, charity, and strong moral fibre. The reader who wants to know Lincoln's mind and heart and everyday habits will find them here, presented so skilfully, so felicitously, that he may not at first perceive the authority that characterizes every sentence. In short this book, for all its modesty, is one of the finest and most durable of this century's Lincoln studies.

Mrs. Lincoln

W. A. EVANS.
MRS. ABRAHAM LINCOLN. 1932.

Dr. Evans, a wise and well informed physician, wrote this book to answer a series of questions that had long puzzled him. A study of Lincoln's life had set him to reflecting on Mrs. Lincoln's share of the responsibility for her husband's advance from obscurity to prominence. To form even a theory, he soon discovered, was almost impossible: whole libraries dealt with the life of Lincoln, but contained almost nothing concerning his wife. The dearth of material added fascination to the subject. "What," Dr. Evans asked himself, "was Mrs. Lincoln's type of mind? What were her personality traits? How did she come by these traits and how did she acquire her mental qualities? How much of them did she inherit? What experiences and influences of her childhood contributed to her personality? What in her make-up is explained by the experiences of her life as a girl in Kentucky, and as a marriageable young woman in Springfield society? What were the effects of her experiences as a married woman and a mother in Springfield? As the wife of a president? What influences did health, religion, politics, financial problems, society, have on her? Was she altered by successes and failures in any of these fields? Did she change radically as she went along the highway of life? Was she more responsible for what she did at one time than another?"

These questions constitute an outline of Dr. Evans's book. With the sympathetic objectivity of a physician in the consulting room he assembles the evidence on every phase of Mrs. Lincoln's life, and then assesses its significance. Her ancestry, he finds, contributed much to her personality, including a tendency, transmitted through her mother, to abnormality. In childhood she did not receive the training in restraint and relaxation—or, receiving it, failed to profit by it—that might have held her stable throughout maturity. As a girl and young woman she was schooled in the social graces but not in the assumption of responsibility. Nevertheless, she came through the Springfield period of her marriage without any noticeable deterioration of personality. But after 1861 she was subjected to terrific stresses —the death of Willie, the assassination of her husband, the burden of secret debt, Tad's death. Her mind collapsed.

Mrs. Lincoln was adjudged insane in 1875. A year later she was declared competent. Dr. Evans, however, holds that she was not accountable for all her actions between 1861 and 1865, and that after Lincoln's death she was irresponsible.

Critics may not always agree with Dr. Evans's evaluation of his evidence, but there can be no objections to his main conclusions.

CARL SANDBURG AND PAUL M. ANGLE.
  MARY LINCOLN, WIFE AND WIDOW. 1932.

Evans's *Mrs. Abraham Lincoln* is a medical man's analysis of a personality: *Mary Lincoln, Wife and Widow* is biography. But it is biography with unusual features. Part One is a sketch of Mrs. Lincoln done with all the insight and artistry that one expects from Carl Sandburg; Part Two consists of the principal documents on which his interpretation is based. Thus the reader, possessed of all the essential materials, can check, and correct if he chooses, the author's conclusions.

Sandburg's account of Lincoln's marriage seemed to call for more detailed substantiation than either text or footnotes could afford. This substantiation Angle supplied in a twenty-page Appendix. There it is contended: (1) that Herndon's account of Lincoln's failure to appear at his wedding is pure fiction, (2) that Matilda Edwards had no responsibility for the broken engagement, and (3) that Sarah Rickard had been the object of attention from Speed instead of from Lincoln, as has been universally believed. These contentions have not yet been seriously challenged.

ELIZABETH KECKLEY.
  BEHIND THE SCENES. 1868.

Under this title Mrs. Lincoln's colored dressmaker told the story of her own life, and more particularly, the story of her association with Mrs. Lincoln during the latter's residence in the White House and for several years afterward.

Elizabeth Keckley, a former slave who had bought her own freedom, was a woman of character and intelligence, and Mrs. Lincoln soon made her a confidante. As time passed, the dressmaker became the closest friend of the President's wife. It was she for whom Mrs. Lincoln sent on the night of Lincoln's assassination, and to whom she turned for aid when she made her fatuous decision to raise funds by selling her own wardrobe.

The book is obviously ghost-written,[8] yet even this fact, ordinarily damaging, does not impair one's confidence in its essential truthfulness. The author's delineation of Mrs. Lincoln's character has been fully corroborated by later publications, while her account of the wardrobe episode rests on documents the genuineness of which is beyond question. Some allowance should doubtless be made for exaggeration, but the book cannot be heavily discounted, no matter how reluctant one may be to accept its revelations.

A new edition, published in 1931, adds nothing to the original.

Finances

HARRY E. PRATT.
THE PERSONAL FINANCES OF ABRAHAM LINCOLN. 1943.

Genuinely original contributions to Lincoln literature are rare. This is one.

Pratt proves—and "proves" is what is meant—that the

[8] See *Lincoln Lore*, March 23, 1936.

fondly-held tradition of Lincoln's poverty has little basis in
fact. It is true that his family was poor during his boyhood
and youth, but there is nothing to indicate that his parents
were any worse off financially than most pioneers. It is also
true that as a young merchant Lincoln indulged in some
shoestring financing that left him loaded with debt, but
within a few years he cleaned up his obligations, and never
thereafter was he pressed for money. His law practice
provided a comfortable living and gave him a surplus
to invest in notes and mortgage loans. By the time of his
election in 1860 he was worth $15,000 or thereabouts—
and in 1860 that was the equivalent of several times that
sum today.

By meticulous research, Pratt shows that Lincoln in-
vested nearly two thirds of his presidential salary of $25,000
a year in government bonds. David Davis, his administrator, found assets of $83,000; by skilful handling he
increased that amount to $111,000 by the end of 1867,
when the estate was distributed to Mrs. Lincoln and the two
surviving sons.

Pratt's book is primarily factual, yet it makes a point:
Lincoln was not greatly interested in the accumulation of
wealth, but he knew the importance of money and safe-
guarded what he had with the conservatism that was one of
his cardinal traits.

An Appendix includes several of Lincoln's accounts with
Springfield merchants, his Springfield bank account, and a
summary of Mrs. Lincoln's financial situation in widow-
hood. Numerous illustrations add authority and interest to
the text.

Health

WILLIAM F. PETERSEN.
   LINCOLN-DOUGLAS: THE WEATHER AS
   DESTINY. 1943.

Dr. Petersen is convinced that the weather—sun, rain, heat, cold, atmospheric pressure—exercises a much greater influence on health than is commonly believed. To illustrate his thesis, and bring it to the notice of the general reader, he has applied it to the lives of Lincoln, Mrs. Lincoln, and Stephen A. Douglas.

Lincoln was a good example of the linear type of human being—tall, thin, without the reserves of fat, sugar, and vitamins that make for energy and endurance. Douglas was his opposite—short, broad, and muscular—and so was Mary Todd. The two types are as dissimilar chemically as physically, and they react to their environment in different ways. Thus Lincoln was likely to be tired and vacillating in the cool damp days of spring, while the same season left Douglas buoyant and energetic. The summer's heat gave Lincoln vigor and poise, and left Douglas in exhaustion. Temperamentally, the linear type runs to introspection; short stocky men are usually extroverts.

Into this hypothesis Lincoln's reactions in specific crises fit neatly. Why did Ann Rutledge's death bring him to the verge of insanity? Emotional strain played a big part, but Dr. Petersen holds that a sudden summer cold wave was not without its influence. Why did Lincoln break his engagement with Mary Todd on January 1, 1841? Because on that day the thermometer suddenly plunged below zero, and on a very cold day a tall man's blood vessels will be constricted, his blood pressure will fall, and his mood will be one of bleak despair. Why were Lincoln and Mary Todd reconciled and married in the fall of 1842? October was a beautiful month, with rising temperatures and many clear days. In such weather a man of Lincoln's type gains confidence, while to Mary Todd, his opposite, the tranquil autumn days would have brought both biological and temperamental stability.

These are only a few of the examples which Dr. Petersen cites and supports with data from meteorological records, contemporary letters and diaries, and reminiscences. He does not claim that his is a complete explanation of Lincoln's motives, and he states frankly that he is only incidentally interested "in making apparent why Lincoln would react in a certain fashion to a certain situation or why Douglas might react in an opposite way." Nevertheless, his hypothesis must be taken into account by anyone who is interested in Lincoln's springs of behavior, and those who have no interest in motivation will find enough about health and environment in this book to make it worth their attention.

Literary Art

DANIEL KILHAM DODGE.
ABRAHAM LINCOLN, MASTER OF
WORDS. 1924.

The chapter headings of *Abraham Lincoln, Master of Words* show that a small book can cover a broad subject:

Speeches in the Illinois Legislature and in Congress
On the Platform and in Congress
1852–1858
From the "Cooper Institute Address" to the "Second Inaugural"
The "Gettysburg Address"
Messages and Proclamations .
Lectures and Occasional Addresses
Letters and Telegrams

In spite of its scope, Professor Dodge's study is anything but superficial. In the case of Lincoln's two inaugural addresses he not only made his own critical analysis of their form and content, but also noted the reception accorded to them by typical newspapers. With the Gettysburg Address he went even further, noting the great variations in the text as the nation's press presented it. His appreciative appraisal of Lincoln's messages to Congress and of the presidential proclamations, generally ignored by other writers, constitutes an outstanding chapter.

Abraham Lincoln, Master of Words invites comparison with Luther E. Robinson's *Abraham Lincoln As a Man of Letters*, published six years earlier. Robinson's book, though worth reading, lacks both the critical acumen and incisiveness of Dodge's study.

Temperance

WILLIAM H. TOWNSEND.
LINCOLN AND LIQUOR. 1934.

At first blush, Lincoln's attitude toward the problems growing out of man's fondness for alcoholic liquor may seem to be of something less than cosmic importance. The subject, however, is one which was long monopolized by those who were more interested in making a case than in learning the truth. The problems, moreover, persist. There is every likelihood that partisans will continue to cite Lincoln's example in support of their own contentions, while bewildered citizens ask, as Mr. Townsend asks in his Preface:

"Would he [Lincoln] favor state-wide prohibition, or would he endorse the view of those who contend that temperance is a personal matter which can not be enforced by legislation? Was Lincoln a total abstainer, a prohibitionist, and a lecturer against the evils of strong drink, or was he a user of liquor, a saloonkeeper in his early manhood, and a foe of reform who denounced prohibition as a 'species of intemperance within itself'?"

To the first of these questions Mr. Townsend has offered no answer, but the others he settles unequivocally. Here are the facts about the use of liquor in Kentucky and Indiana during Lincoln's boyhood; here is his record on liquor questions as they came before the Illinois legislature while he was a member; here his personal habits are established with authority; and here are the authentic references he made to temperance questions while he was President.

In spite of a few minor errors—for example, the author's acceptance at face value of the spurious letter to George E. Pickett[9]—it is probable that *Lincoln and Liquor* will remain standard for many years to come.

[9] See p. 8.

Religion

WILLIAM E. BARTON.
THE SOUL OF ABRAHAM LINCOLN. 1920.

Nearly everything that has been written about Lincoln's religion is either controversial or biased. That fact adds value to *The Soul of Abraham Lincoln* which, though the work of a minister, represents a sincere effort to present only clearly substantiated facts.

Dr. Barton sought to establish the truth by four lines of inquiry. In the first section of his book he developed the religious background of Lincoln's life—the practices and affiliations of his parents in Kentucky and Indiana, the New Salem environment, the degree of his own observance while living in Springfield and Washington. Next he selected, presented, and criticized the evidence bearing on Lincoln's own convictions. Here is to be found such testimony as that of Newton Bateman, Ward H. Lamon, William H. Herndon, and Daniel E. Sickles. His third approach was the negative one of ascertaining what Lincoln was by demonstrating what he was not. He was not, for example, an atheist, nor a spiritualist, nor a Quaker. Finally, he selected passages from Lincoln's writings which show religious convictions of a high order, and out of these formulated what he described as Lincoln's creed. An Appendix contains considerable pertinent material—excerpts from Bateman, Herndon, Nicolay & Hay; the Rev. James A. Reed's lecture on Lincoln's religion; B. F. Irwin's article on the same subject.

In the twenty-five years which have passed since this book was published many pages have been added to the theme. In fullness and authority, however, *The Soul of Abraham Lincoln* still stands by itself.

Photographs and Cartoons

FREDERICK HILL MESERVE AND CARL SANDBURG.
THE PHOTOGRAPHS OF ABRAHAM
LINCOLN. 1944.

In 1911 F. H. Meserve established his authority in the field of Lincoln photographs by publishing a book with the same title as the one noticed here. That book, however, has long been in need of revision. Over the years new facts have come to light, correcting many of Meserve's dates and descriptions, and twenty photographs were added to the one hundred originally presented. Moreover, the first publication, limited to 100 copies, has long been practically unobtainable, and since it was sumptuously printed, with photographic prints instead of reproductions, the price of the few copies that have changed hands has been far beyond the means of all but large libraries or well-to-do collectors.

In the Meserve and Sandburg publication the original Meserve has been brought up to date. All necessary corrections in the text have been made; the recently-discovered photographs have been added, and so have one hundred pictures of members of Lincoln's family, old friends, high army officers, and prominent government officials. By resorting to half-tone reproductions—not, unfortunately, very good ones—the price of the book has been brought within the means of any buyer.

In addition to pictures and captions there are two essays by Sandburg—one on the face of Lincoln, the other a biographical appreciation of Meserve—and an essay by Meserve on Lincoln photographs.

STEFAN LORANT.
    LINCOLN, HIS LIFE IN PHOTOGRAPHS. 1941.

Essentially, this is a juvenile picture book. In it are more than four hundred pictures. Included are pictures of the cabins and houses in which Lincoln lived, the members of his family, the members of his cabinet, the principal Civil War commanders, and some photographs of events—notably both inaugurations, the dedication of the military cemetery at Gettysburg, and the hanging of the Lincoln conspirators. Many facsimiles of letters and documents help to carry the narrative. A valuable feature is the publication of all the photographic portraits of Lincoln.

Many of the Lincoln photographs are beautifully reproduced, and superb in their realistic detail. The presentation, in fact, is much more effective than that achieved by the publishers of Meserve and Sandburg.

In some respects, however, Mr. Lorant was unfortunate. There is no photograph of Thomas Lincoln, the President's father, in spite of the picture so captioned on p. 15; and the facsimile, on p. 62, of the letter to Mrs. Bixby is a reproduction of a fabrication. (The text of the letter is genuine.)

Mr. Lorant was also unfortunate, or uninformed, in many of his captions, while the biographical narrative is even more immature than the nature of the book made advisable.

To sum up: young readers, unconcerned about strict accuracy, should enjoy *Lincoln, His Life in Photographs* in its entirety; adults will be interested principally in the photographs.

ALBERT SHAW.
ABRAHAM LINCOLN: A CARTOON HISTORY. 1929.

The cartoons and other illustrations in this two-volume work are not very well reproduced; many are not identified as to source; the text is long, discursive, and often dull. Nevertheless, cartoons are valuable reflections of public opinion, and this is the only reasonably satisfactory collection of the cartoons of Lincoln's time.

Volume One bears the title, *Abraham Lincoln: His Path to the Presidency*, and covers the years from Lincoln's birth to 1860. Because Lincoln did not become a national figure until the very end of this period, the author had to depend for illustrative material on photographs of places with which Lincoln was identified and on cartoons which depict the national political situation without reference to Lincoln. In Volume Two, *Abraham Lincoln: The Year of His Election*, Lincoln is the principal subject of the caricaturists.

The book does not include the period of Lincoln's presidency.

The Assassination

David Miller DeWitt.
   THE ASSASSINATION OF ABRAHAM
   LINCOLN. 1909.

Since 1909 a small library has been written about Lincoln's assassination and its aftermath. Nevertheless, this book has not been superseded. In fact, in some respects it remains the most reasonable and best balanced treatment of the whole tangled subject.

DeWitt, whose passion it was to subject controversial questions of history to judicial analysis,[10] begins his narrative with the abortive plot to capture Lincoln. There follows the story of the assassination, Booth's capture and death, the trial of the conspirators, their sentencing and execution. Then come a relentless critique of the military commission's competence, an account of the disintegration of the conspiracy charge against the responsible leaders of the Confederacy, the almost incredible tale of the escape of John H. Surratt and his tardy trial, and finally, a penetrating exposé of the suppression of the plea for clemency that might have saved Mrs. Surratt from the gallows.

Although DeWitt wrote without benefit of considerable evidence that later students have used, his close scrutiny of the published records led him to what were then startling conclusions and caused him to ask disturbing questions. In Stanton he saw not the fierce patriot of the orthodox his-

[10]He was also the author of *The Judicial Murder of Mary E. Surratt* (1895), and *The Impeachment and Trial of Andrew Johnson* (1903).

torians, but a "pilot more unfit to ride the whirlwind and direct the storm" than any other who could have been found—a man so deficient in self-control "that a rational and equitable judgment was the one thing he could not keep cool long enough to form." The military commission, he concluded, had been without legal jurisdiction over the conspirators, yet it had sent four of them to death and four to life imprisonment. The alleged involvement of high Confederate officials in Lincoln's murder takes on ludicrous aspects under his telling. Other matters have no comic aspect. What happened to the pages missing in Booth's diary? Why was the government so unwilling to have John H. Surratt apprehended and brought to trial that it acted only when action could no longer be evaded? Who suppressed the petition asking clemency for Mrs. Surratt, and who lied and who told the truth about that shady episode?

One should not conclude, from this summary, that sensation is the essence of DeWitt's book. On the contrary, sobriety is its chief characteristic—sobriety and well proportioned, well founded narrative. The startling conclusions and implications are only the inevitable results of the operation of an honest, questioning mind, undeterred by the historian's besetting fear of passing judgment.

DeWitt's notes, relegated to an Appendix, deserve the attention of every careful student.

OTTO EISENSCHIML.
WHY WAS LINCOLN MURDERED? 1937.

David Miller DeWitt studied the open record of the conspiracy trial and came up with a number of conclusions and questions that reflect seriously upon men who held high office in the government of the United States. Otto Eisenschiml went far beyond the open record—to the archives of the War Department, the records of the Capital police, to all private papers which patient, sustained research could locate—and emerged with conclusions and questions and mysterious circumstances in comparison with which the contentions of DeWitt become few and almost orthodox. About all one is sure of after reading Eisenschiml is that on the 14th of April, 1865, John Wilkes Booth shot Abraham Lincoln; that twelve days later a man who may have been Booth was shot in the Garrett barn; and that in due though improper course seven men and one woman were convicted of complicity in the crime and either hanged or sent to prison.

To illustrate: Eisenschiml shows that Stanton knew the identity of Lincoln's assassin long before midnight on April 14, yet he did not make Booth's name public until 3:00 A.M. on the 15th. And in spite of the fact that Booth was almost certain to strike for Richmond, news of Lincoln's assassination was not published in that city until April 17, even though there was ready communication with Washington at all times.

To illustrate further: Soon after the assassination every road out of the capital was barred—except the road to Port Tobacco. Yet this was the road the assassin was most likely to take! Moreover, within a few hours of Lincoln's murder, the War Department knew that Booth and Herold had crossed the Anacostia Bridge and at least started on this road. Nevertheless, no troops were sent in pursuit, and when an enterprising officer asked for cavalry horses so that he might dispatch a detail over the Port Tobacco Road, his request was refused.

Eisenschiml has singled out many ominous circumstances in addition to those mentioned, and he has not hesitated to imply that they are not all the result of accident or ineptitude. The reader is bound to infer that the Radical Republicans, and Edwin M. Stanton especially, were responsible for Lincoln's death, although Eisenschiml carefully points out that no scrap of positive evidence supports this hypothesis. Every student would do well to keep that warning in mind.

One may or may not accept the author's implied solution of his mystery. His facts, however, remain—startling enough to be worth following for their own sake. They reveal, at the least, almost unbelievable inefficiency in the War Department, and go far to explain why four years passed before the North was able to subdue a South greatly inferior in both men and resources.

GEORGE S. BRYAN.
THE GREAT AMERICAN MYTH. 1940.

The story of Lincoln's murder, Mr. Bryan held, had become the center of a congeries of lies, errors, inventions, and delusions unequalled in American history. Therefore he concluded that the time had come for a new recital of the facts, uncolored by theories of diabolism, and for a retelling of the life-story of John Wilkes Booth. *The Great American Myth* resulted.

The book might well be described as the official version of Lincoln's murder. In it Booth, who, Bryan holds, was a very good actor, and not the third-rate ranter whom several recent writers have described, is the villain. It was he who killed Lincoln, and on his own responsibility. Moreover, it was Booth who was captured and mortally wounded in the Garrett barn. The contention that Stanton was involved in the crime, and that he hoped to make Booth's escape possible, Bryan dismisses as a theory both "inapt" and "malicious."

This is not to say that *The Great American Myth* is simply a retelling of the old familiar story. Mr. Bryan has re-affirmed its main outlines, but only after a painstaking evaluation of the evidence, some of it new. Many, neverthe-less, will not accept his version as the last word, nor can they be censured for their skepticism. For one thing, the material for proving certain cardinal points in the story of Lincoln's murder simply does not exist. In the second place, Mr. Bryan failed to deal adequately with several important questions—notably the existence of a conspiracy to assas-sinate Lincoln, and the problem of Mrs. Surratt's guilt and Dr. Mudd's complicity. These, however, are minor inade-quacies. Many readers will consider them more than atoned for by the author's refusal to see more than an occasional evil-spirit lurking in the shadows.

Legends

Lloyd Lewis.

MYTHS AFTER LINCOLN. 1929.

This is one of the most original, most provocative, most readable books in Lincoln literature.

In the assassination of Lincoln and in his heroic fame Lewis sees the pattern of an age-old folk belief—the myth of the dying god. The martyr, usually of lowly origin, is the kind and gentle benefactor who pours out his blood that his people may prosper. After death his divinity becomes apparent. Usually his ascent to immortality is accomplished through the agency of a Judas or a Modred, who achieves undying notoriety. Often, too, the villain is reputed to live long after his reported death—a quick and certain end is too easy a punishment to be credible.

Within this framework Lewis tells the story of Lincoln's death and traces the rise of his legendary fame. Few well established historical sequences contain more dark and bizarre episodes. There was the cry for vengeance that rose from a thousand pulpits on "Black Easter" to make a mockery of Lincoln's plans for reunion; the long drawn-out funeral pageant from Washington to Springfield; the blundering that resulted in the execution of Mrs. Surratt; the attempted theft of Lincoln's body; the reported survival of not one but several Booths; the eventual madness of a number of those who were involved in Lincoln's death. These and other strange circumstances fed and fortified the legend until it became the tale of the one and indubitable American god.

Myths After Lincoln is a study in folklore, but it makes a historical contribution of first importance. Nowhere else is the North's abrupt reversal from leniency to harshness towards the South so vividly portrayed. Knowing that reversal and the causes of it, one understands better the tragic years of the Reconstruction Period.

ROY P. BASLER.

THE LINCOLN LEGEND. 1935.

This book traces the changing conception of Lincoln as expressed in biography, fiction, poetry, and sculpture. Basler's interest is not limited to the Lincoln of historical fact, although he knows that Lincoln well; it extends to the man whom John Drinkwater, Thomas Dixon, and Walt Whitman—to name only the smallest number—delineated. His chapter headings are revealing. "A Survey of Lincoln Literature" covers the general subject summarily; "The Diviners of Lincoln" deals with the conceptions of Lincoln held by contemporaries like Horace Greeley, Wendell Phillips, James Russell Lowell, and Charles Eliot Norton; "Between Folklore and Fiction" is concerned with such partly factual, partly legendary phases of Lincoln's life and character as his honesty, his capacity as a woodsman, and his love for Ann Rutledge; the popular attribution of Christ-like qualities to Lincoln is the subject of the chapter entitled "The Prophet, Savior, and Martyr"; "Emancipation and Savior of the Union" needs no explanation; and "The American" is the identification, by the poets, of Lincoln with the ideal representative of American democracy.

In Basler's own words, his purpose was "to show how poets, writers of fiction, dramatists, and occasionally biographers have, with the help of the folk-mind, created about Lincoln a national legend or myth which in conception is much like the hero-myths of other nations." The author, however, never quite lives up to his promise, or perhaps it would be more accurate to say that he fails to make his point sharply and impressively. As a result, many readers will be more impressed by the book's value as an anthology and guide to Lincoln fiction, poetry, and drama, than by its thesis. That thesis, nevertheless, is a novel and important one, and should not be disregarded merely because Basler's treatment of it is not wholly convincing.

Bibliography

JAY MONAGHAN.
LINCOLN BIBLIOGRAPHY, 1839–1939. 1945.

This bibliography, appearing eighty years after Lincoln's death, is the first scholarly listing of the voluminous literature that deals with his career.

Fundamental in an appraisal of any bibliography is the author's definition of its scope. Here is Monaghan's:

> All printed books and pamphlets dealing principally with (1) Abraham Lincoln (2) his ancestry (3) his wife, children, step-mother and sister (but excluding material relating to the individual career of Robert T. Lincoln) or (4) having the name of Abraham Lincoln prominently in their titles; excluding all material appearing in periodicals and separates of periodical articles printed for private distribution by the author of the article, unless title page, type or pagination are different from the original printing, and unless prefatory material has been added; excluding all general histories of the United States, of the Civil War, or of Illinois, no matter how prominent the part of Lincoln in them; excluding all published sources dealing incidentally with Lincoln's life, such as the Welles and Browning diaries; excluding all distinctly advertising bulletins, pamphlets, and pictures, menus, programs of school exercises, etc., except where they contain sufficient informational material to render them of permanent value.

This is substantially the definition adopted by Daniel

Fish and J. B. Oakleaf, Monaghan's principal predecessors in the field of Lincoln bibliography, but where they permitted themselves many departures and exceptions, he held himself rigidly within his limits. As a result, he excluded some 350 titles listed in their books. Even so, his total runs to 3,958 items, or 896 more than are to be found in the combined works of Fish, Oakleaf, and John W. Starr, Jr.

Other differences between the work of Monaghan and the bibliographies of his predecessors are even more significant. His arrangement is chronological rather than alphabetical. Each item is described, whereas all earlier bibliographers contented themselves with transcriptions of titles. Location symbols show where at least one copy of every item is to be found, and all known copies of extremely rare items are located. Title pages of works in such languages as Russian and Chinese are reproduced as illustrations.

The book contains a detailed index, an introduction in which the author traces the history of Lincoln bibliography, and a foreword by J. G. Randall.

Bibliography

THIS bibliography lists only those books which are the subjects of separate appraisals in this volume. Books to which no more than casual reference is made are not included. The arrangement is alphabetical according to author. Collections of Lincoln's writings and other compilations are entered under the names of the editors. In most instances, the full bibliographical description is given for the first trade edition only.

Angle, Paul M. *New Letters and Papers of Lincoln.* Boston: Houghton Mifflin, 1930.

Angle, Paul M. *Lincoln, 1854–1861; Being the Day-by-Day Activities of Abraham Lincoln from January 1, 1854 to March 4, 1861.* Springfield, Illinois: Abraham Lincoln Association, 1933.

Angle, Paul M. *"Here I Have Lived": A History of Lincoln's Springfield, 1821–1865.* Springfield, Illinois: Abraham Lincoln Association, 1935.

Arnold, Isaac N. *The Life of Abraham Lincoln.* Chicago: Jansen, McClurg & Co., 1885.

Ballard, Colin R. *The Military Genius of Abraham Lincoln.* London: Oxford University Press, 1926.

Baringer, William E. *Lincoln's Rise to Power.* Boston: Little, Brown. 1937.

Baringer, William E. *A House Dividing: Lincoln as President Elect.* Springfield, Illinois: Abraham Lincoln Association, 1945.

Barton, William E. *The Paternity of Abraham Lincoln: Was He the Son of Thomas Lincoln? An Essay on the Chastity of Nancy Hanks.* New York: Doran, 1920.

Barton, William E. *The Soul of Abraham Lincoln.* New York: Doran, 1920.

Barton, William E. *The Life of Abraham Lincoln.* Two vols. Indianapolis: Bobbs-Merrill, 1925.

Barton, William E. *The Lineage of Lincoln.* Indianapolis: Bobbs-Merrill, 1929.

Barton, William E. *Lincoln at Gettysburg: What He Intended to Say; What He Said; What He Was Reported to Have Said; What He Wished He Had Said.* Indianapolis: Bobbs-Merrill, 1930.

Basler, Roy P. *The Lincoln Legend: A Study in Changing Conceptions.* Boston: Houghton Mifflin, 1935.

Basler, Roy P. *Abraham Lincoln: His Speeches and Writings*. Cleveland: World Publishing Co., 1946.

Beveridge, Albert J. *Abraham Lincoln, 1809–1858*. Two vols. Boston: Houghton Mifflin, 1928.

Brooks, Noah. *Washington in Lincoln's Time*. New York: Century Co., 1895.

Browne, Francis Fisher. *The Every-day Life of Abraham Lincoln*. New York and St. Louis: N. D. Thompson Pub. Co., 1886. Preference is given to the revised edition, Chicago: Browne & Howell Co., 1913.

Bryan, George S. *The Great American Myth*. New York: Carrick & Evans, 1940.

Carman, Harry J., and Luthin, Reinhard H. *Lincoln and the Patronage*. New York: Columbia University Press, 1943.

Carpenter, Francis B. *Six Months at the White House with Abraham Lincoln: The Story of a Picture*. New York: Hurd and Houghton, 1866. Editions 1868 and later appeared under the title, *The Inner Life of Abraham Lincoln: Six Months at the White House*.

Charnwood, Lord Godfrey Rathbone Benson. *Abraham Lincoln*. London: Constable & Co., 1916. First American edition: New York: Holt, 1917.

Daugherty, James. *Abraham Lincoln*. New York: Viking Press, 1943.

Dennett, Tyler. *Lincoln and the Civil War in the Diaries and Letters of John Hay*. New York: Dodd, Mead & Co., 1939.

DeWitt, David Miller. *The Assassination of Abraham Lincoln and its Expiation*. New York: Macmillan, 1909.

Dodge, Daniel K. *Abraham Lincoln, Master of Words*. New York: Appleton, 1924.

Eisenschiml, Otto. *Why Was Lincoln Murdered?* Boston: Little, Brown, 1937.

Evans, William A. *Mrs. Abraham Lincoln: A Study of Her Personality and Her Influence on Lincoln*. New York: Knopf, 1932.

Herndon, William H., and Weik, Jesse W. *Herndon's Lincoln: The True Story of a Great Life*. Three vols. Chicago: Belford, Clarke & Co., 1889. A verbatim reprint of this edition, also in three volumes, was issued in 1921 by the Herndon's Lincoln Publishing Co., Springfield, Ill. The revised edition, two volumes, was first published by D. Appleton and Co., New York, 1892. The latest edition, with introduction and notes by Paul M. Angle, was issued in one volume by Albert & Charles Boni, New York, 1930, and has the title: *Herndon's Life of*

Lincoln: The History and Personal Recollections of Abraham Lincoln as Originally Written by William H. Herndon and Jesse W. Weik.

Hertz, Emanuel. *Abraham Lincoln, A New Portrait.* Two vols. New York: Liveright, 1931.

Hertz, Emanuel. *The Hidden Lincoln, From the Letters and Papers of William H. Herndon.* New York: Viking Press, 1938.

Holland, Josiah G. *The Life of Abraham Lincoln.* Springfield, Mass.: Gurdon Bill, 1866.

Howells, William Dean. *Life of Abraham Lincoln.* Springfield, Ill.: Abraham Lincoln Association, 1938. As noted in the text, this is a reproduction of the first part of Howells' 1860 campaign biography made from a copy which Lincoln himself corrected.

Keckley, Elizabeth. *Behind the Scenes.* New York: Carleton & Co., 1868. Reprinted: Buffalo: Stansil and Lee, 1931.

Lamon, Ward Hill. *The Life of Abraham Lincoln; From His Birth to His Inauguration as President.* Boston: Osgood & Co., 1872.

Learned, Marion D. *Abraham Lincoln, An American Migration: Family English Not German.* Philadelphia: William J. Campbell, 1909.

Lewis, Lloyd. *Myths After Lincoln.* New York: Harcourt, Brace, 1929.

Lincoln, Waldo. *History of the Lincoln Family: An Account of the Descendants of Samuel Lincoln of Hingham Massachusetts 1637–1920.* Worcester, Mass.: Commonwealth Press, 1923.

Lorant, Stefan. *Lincoln: His Life in Photographs.* New York: Duell, Sloan and Pearce, 1941.

Luthin, Reinhard H. *The First Lincoln Campaign.* Cambridge: Harvard University Press, 1944.

McCarthy, Charles H. *Lincoln's Plan of Reconstruction.* New York: McClure, Phillips & Co., 1901.

McClure, Alexander K. *Abraham Lincoln and Men of War-times: Some Personal Recollections of War and Politics during the Lincoln Administration.* Philadelphia: Times Publishing Co., 1892.

Meserve, Frederick Hill, and Sandburg, Carl. *The Photographs of Abraham Lincoln.* New York: Harcourt, Brace, 1944.

Monaghan, Jay. *Lincoln Bibliography, 1839–1939.* Two vols. (Collections of the Illinois State Historical Library, Vols. 31 and 32.) Springfield, Ill.: Illinois State Historical Library, 1943, 1945.

Monaghan, Jay. *Diplomat in Carpet Slippers: Abraham Lincoln Deals with Foreign Affairs.* Indianapolis: Bobbs-Merrill, 1945.

Newton, Joseph Fort. *Lincoln and Herndon.* Cedar Rapids, Iowa: Torch Press, 1910.

Nicolay, Helen. *Personal Traits of Abraham Lincoln.* New York: Century Co., 1912.

Nicolay, John G. *A Short Life of Abraham Lincoln, Condensed from Nicolay & Hay's Abraham Lincoln: A History.* New York: Century Co., 1902.

Nicolay, John G., and Hay, John. *Abraham Lincoln: A History.* Ten vols. New York: Century Co., 1890.

Nicolay, John G., and Hay, John. *Abraham Lincoln, Complete Works: Comprising His Speeches, Letters, State Papers, and Miscellaneous Writings.* Two vols. New York: Century Co., 1894.

Nicolay, John G., and Hay, John. *Complete Works of Abraham Lincoln.* "New and Enlarged Edition." Twelve vols. New York: Francis D. Tandy Co., 1905.

Petersen, William F. *Lincoln—Douglas: The Weather as Destiny.* Springfield, Ill.: Charles C. Thomas, 1943.

Phillips, Isaac N. *Abraham Lincoln By Some Men Who Knew Him.* Bloomington, Ill.: Pantagraph Printing & Stationery Co., 1910.

Potter, David M. *Lincoln and His Party in the Secession Crisis.* New Haven: Yale University Press, 1942.

Pratt, Harry E. *Lincoln, 1840–1846; Being the Day-by-Day Activities of Abraham Lincoln from January 1, 1840 to December 31, 1846.* Springfield, Ill.: Abraham Lincoln Association, 1939.

Pratt, Harry E. *Lincoln, 1809–1839; Being the Day-by-Day Activities of Abraham Lincoln from February 12, 1809 to December 31, 1839.* Springfield, Ill.: Abraham Lincoln Association, 1941.

Pratt, Harry E. *The Personal Finances of Abraham Lincoln.* Springfield, Ill.: Abraham Lincoln Association, 1943.

Randall, James G. *Constitutional Problems Under Lincoln.* New York: Appleton, 1926.

Randall, James G. *Lincoln the President.* Two vols. New York: Dodd, Mead & Co., 1945.

Reep, Thomas P. *Lincoln at New Salem.* Petersburg, Ill.: Old Salem Lincoln League, 1927. (Not to be confused with the same author's earlier and much less desirable *Lincoln and New Salem.*)

Rice, Charles Allen Thorndike. *Reminiscences of Abraham Lincoln by Distinguished Men of His Time.* New York: North American Publishing Co., 1886. Revised edition: New York: Harper & Brothers, 1909.

Sandburg, Carl. *Abraham Lincoln: The Prairie Years.* Two vols. New York: Harcourt, Brace, 1926.

Sandburg, Carl. *Abraham Lincoln: The War Years.* Four vols. New York: Harcourt, Brace, 1939.

Sandburg, Carl, and Angle, Paul M. *Mary Lincoln, Wife and Widow.* New York: Harcourt, Brace, 1932.

Shaw, Albert. *Abraham Lincoln: His Path to the Presidency.* Two vols. New York: Review of Reviews Corp., 1929. (Vol. Two is entitled *Abraham Lincoln: The Year of His Election.*)

Sparks, Edwin Erle. *The Lincoln-Douglas Debates of 1858.* (Collections of the Illinois State Historical Library, Vol. Three.) Springfield, Ill.: Illinois State Historical Library, 1908.

Stephenson, Nathaniel W. *Lincoln: An Account of His Personal Life, Especially of its Springs of Action as Revealed and Deepened by the Ordeal of War.* Indianapolis: Bobbs-Merrill, 1922.

Stern, Philip Van Doren. *The Life and Writings of Abraham Lincoln.* New York: Random House, 1940. Revised edition: New York: Modern Library, 1942.

Tarbell, Ida M. *The Life of Abraham Lincoln.* Two vols. New York: McClure, Phillips & Co., 1900.

Tarbell, Ida M. *In the Footsteps of the Lincolns.* New York: Harper & Bros., 1924.

Thomas, Benjamin P. *Lincoln's New Salem.* Springfield, Ill.: Abraham Lincoln Association, 1934.

Thomas, Benjamin P. *Lincoln, 1847–1853; Being the Day-by-Day Activities of Abraham Lincoln from January 1, 1847 to December 31, 1853.* Springfield, Ill.: Abraham Lincoln Association, 1936.

Townsend, William H. *Lincoln and His Wife's Home Town.* Indianapolis: Bobbs-Merrill, 1929.

Townsend, William H. *Lincoln and Liquor.* New York: Press of the Pioneers, 1934.

Tracy, Gilbert A. *Uncollected Letters of Abraham Lincoln.* Boston: Houghton Mifflin, 1917.

Warren, Louis A. *Lincoln's Parentage & Childhood: A History of the Kentucky Lincolns Supported by Documentary Evidence.* New York: Century Co., 1926.

Weik, Jesse W. *The Real Lincoln: A Portrait.* Boston: Houghton Mifflin, 1922.

Whitney, Henry C. *Life on the Circuit with Lincoln.* Boston: Estes and Lauriat, 1892. Reprinted, with introduction and notes by Paul M. Angle, Caldwell, Idaho: Caxton Printers, 1940.

Williams, T. Harry. *Lincoln and the Radicals.* Madison: University of Wisconsin Press, 1941.

Wilson, Rufus Rockwell. *Lincoln Among His Friends: A Sheaf of Intimate Memories*. Caldwell, Idaho: Caxton Printers, 1942.

Wilson, Rufus Rockwell. *Intimate Memories of Lincoln*. Elmira, N. Y.: Primavera Press, 1945.

Woldman, Albert A. *Lawyer Lincoln*. Boston: Houghton Mifflin, 1936.

Index

Allen, E. A., offers to sell rifles, 87–88.

Alton Railroad, beginnings, xvi.

Andrews, E. W., reminiscences by, 99.

Angle, Paul M., "*Here I Have Lived*," 75–76; *Lincoln 1854–1861*, 69–72; *New Letters and Papers of Lincoln*, 12–13.

Angle, Paul M., and Sandburg, Carl, *Mary Lincoln, Wife and Widow*, 110.

Arkansas, reconstruction in, 95.

Army of the Potomac, Lincoln visits, 78.

Arnold, Isaac N., *History of Abraham Lincoln and the Overthrow of Slavery*, 24; *Life of Abraham Lincoln*, 24–26.

Ballard, Colin R., *Military Genius of Abraham Lincoln*, 89–90.

Banks, Nathaniel P., political career, 83.

Baringer, William E., *A House Dividing*, 84; *Lincoln's Rise to Power*, 82–83.

Bartlett, Truman H., letters from Herndon, 96.

Barton, William E., on illegitimacy of Nancy Hanks, 32n; *Life of Abraham Lincoln*, 46–49; *Lincoln at Gettysburg*, 94–95; *Lineage of Lincoln*, 65–66; *Paternity of Abraham Lincoln*, 66; *President Lincoln*, 49n; *Soul of Abraham Lincoln*, 117–18.

"Basic Lincolniana," vi.

Basler, Roy P., *Abraham Lincoln: His Speeches and Writings*, 16; *Lincoln Legend*, 127–28.

Bateman, Newton, on Lincoln's religion, 117.

Bates, Edwin, political career, 83.

Beard, Charles A., quoted, 58.

Beecher, Henry Ward, reminiscences by, 99.

Benedict, L. S., 15.

Bergen, Abram, reminiscences by, 103.

Beveridge, Albert J., *Abraham Lincoln*, 53–56; work characterized, 59n.

Bibliography, 128–29.

Bill to Abolish Slavery, 9.

Bixby letter, facsimile, 119.

Black, Chauncey F., writes Lamon's *Lincoln*, 22–23.

"Black Easter," 126.

Black Hawk War, Lincoln in, 72.

Blades, Franklin, 98.

Blair, Francis P., 95.

Bledsoe, Albert T., book review by, 103.

Booth, John Wilkes, alleged survival, 126; and assassination of Lincoln, 121–25.

Breckinridge, John C., sketch of, 77.

Breckinridge, Robert J., sketch of, 77.

Bright, John, sketch of, 93.

Brooks, Noah, reminiscences by, 103; *Washington in Lincoln's Time*, 78–79.

Browne, Francis Fisher, *Every-Day Life of Abraham Lincoln*, 26–28.

Browning, Orville H., Diary, xv, 47, 48n.

Bryan, George S., *Great American Myth*, 124–25.

Bunn, John W., reminiscences by, 98, 105.

Burnside, Ambrose E., 86.

Butler, Benjamin F., letter to, 10; and Radicals, 86; reminiscences by, 99.

Cabinet, selection of, 84, 104.

Camp Yates, xii.

Cameron, Simon, characterized, 61, 101; Lincoln's relations with, 102; political career, 83.

Carman, Harry J., and Luthin, Reinhard H., *Lincoln and the Patronage*, 87–88.

Carpenter, Francis B., *Six Months at the White House*, 100–01.

Century Magazine, 33.

Chancellorsville, Battle of, 78.

Chandler, Zachariah, and Radicals, 86.

Charnwood, Godfrey Rathbone Benson, Lord, *Abraham Lincoln*, 42–44.

Chase, Salmon P., character, xvi; Lincoln's relations with, 102; papers of, 82; political career, 83; and Radicals, 86.

Cincinnati, speech at, 14.

Civil War, cause of, 36–37, 60; constitutional questions, 79; foreign policy, 93–94; in Kentucky, 77; Lincoln's conduct of, 89–90.

Clay, Cassius M., political career, 83; sketch of, 77, 93.

Clay, Henry, sketch, 77.

Clinton, speech at, 9.

Coffin, Charles Carleton, reminiscences by, 99.

Colfax, Schuyler, reminiscences by, 100.

Congress, Lincoln in, 115.

Conkling, James C., reminiscences by, 103.

Constitution, U.S., interpretation of, 90–92.

Cooper Union Speech, 16, 115.

Corporations, memorandum on, 15.

Coughlin, Rev. Charles Edward, x.

Crittenden, John J., letter to, 12; sketch, 77.

Cunningham, James O., reminiscences by, 103.

Curtin, Andrew G., Lincoln's relations with, 102.

Daugherty, James, *Abraham Lincoln*, 62–63.

Davis, David, administrator Lincoln estate, 112; reminiscences by, 105.

Dennett, Tyler, *John Hay: From Poetry to Politics*, 34–35; *Lincoln and the Civil War*, 88–89.

DeWitt, David Miller, *Assassination of Abraham Lincoln*, 121–22; *Impeachment and Trial of Andrew Johnson*, 121n; *Judicial Murder of Mary E. Surratt*, 121n.

Dixon, Thomas, 127.

Dodge, Daniel K., *Abraham Lincoln, Master of Words*, 114–15.

Douglas, Stephen A., characterization, 55; defeats Lincoln, 82; health, 113–14; and Peoria "truce," 70.

Dred Scott decision, 79.

Drinkwater, John, 127.

Edwards, Matilda, 110.

Edwards, Mrs. Ninian W., statements by, 96.

Edwardsville, speech, 10.

Eighth Judicial Circuit, 72, 80.

Eisenschiml, Otto, *Why Was Lincoln Murdered?*, 122–24.

Emerson, Ralph Waldo, sketch, 52.

Evans, William A., *Mrs. Abraham Lincoln*, 108–09.

Everett, Edward, Gettysburg oration, 95.

Ewing, James S., reminiscences by, 98.

First Inaugural Address, 6, 16.

Fish, Daniel, *Lincoln Bibliography*, 10, 129.

Ford, Thomas, *History of Illinois*, xv.

Ford, Worthington C., edits Beveridge *Lincoln*, 54.

Forgeries, detection of, 70.

Fort Dearborn Massacre, xiii.

Fort Pickens, Lincoln's policy, 85.

Fort Sumter, Lincoln's policy, 85.

France, recognition sought by Confederacy, 93.

Fredericksburg, Battle of, 78.

Freeman, Edward A., quoted, 95–96.

Fremont, John C., and Radicals, 86.

Fry, James B., reminiscences by, 100.

Galena, speech, 9.

Garibaldi, Giuseppe, command offered, 93.

Gettysburg Address, best account, 48; complete study of, 94–95; writing of, 26; mentioned, 115.

Gettysburg, Battle of, 78.

Gillespie, Joseph, letters to Herndon, 96.

Gilmore, James R., 95.

Gobright, Lawrence A., reminiscences by, 103.

Grant, Ulysses S., xii, 102.

Great Britain, recognition sought by Confederacy, 93.

Greeley, Horace, attempts to make peace, 95; estimate of Lincoln, 103; interpretation of Lincoln, 127; relations with Lincoln, 102.

Grimsley, Elizabeth Todd, "Six Months in the White House," 47, 48n.

Gulliver, Jonathan P., reminiscences by, 101,

Gurowski, Adam, sketch, 93.

Hanks, Dennis, letters to Herndon, 96.

Hanks, John, statements by, 96.

Hanks, Lucy, mother of Nancy Hanks, 34, 47, 65, 68.

Hanks, Nancy, illiterate, 25; parentage, 30, 34, 47, 65; unmarried, 21.

Hanks family, history, 65–69.

Hardin, John J., letter to, 9.

Hart, Charles Henry, letters from Herndon, 96.

Hay, John, Diary, 88–89; on life in White House, 103.

Hay, John, and Nicolay, John G., *Complete Works* (1894), 3–6; *Complete Works* (1905), 6–11; *Abraham Lincoln: A History*, 33–37.

Hayes, John L., "Life and Speeches of Hannibal Hamlin," 17n.

Hicks, Thomas, reminiscences by, 100.

Hill, Frederick Trevor, *Lincoln the Lawyer*, 79.

Hitchcock, Peter, letter to, 12.

Helper, Hinton Rowan, sketch, 52.

Herndon, William H., biography criticized, 59; correspondence with Parker, 105–06; lectures, 28; on Lincoln's religion, 20, 117; reminiscences by, 101; source materials, 96–97, 105; wedding story, 110.

Herndon, William H., and Weik, Jesse W., *Herndon's Lincoln*, 28–33.

Herold, David, 123.

Hertz, Emanuel, *Abraham Lincoln: A New Portrait*, 13–15; *The Hidden Lincoln*, 29n, 96–97.

Holland, Josiah G., *Life of Abraham Lincoln*, 18–20.

Hooker, Joseph, 86.

House, Albert V., Jr., on Lamon's Recollections, 24; "Trials of a Ghost Writer of Lincoln Biography," 22n.

"House Divided" speech, quoted, 5; mentioned, 16, 82.

Howard, James Quay, 17.

Howells, William Dean, *Life of Abraham Lincoln*, 17–18.

Hoyt, Charles, letter to, 9.

Illinois Central Railroad, xvi.

Illinois Legislature, Lincoln in, 115, 116.

Indiana, Lincoln family in, 72, 73.

Ingersoll, Robert G., reminiscences by, 99.

Irwin, B. F., on Lincoln's religion, 117.

Johnson, Allen, *Stephen A. Douglas*, 3.

Johnson, Andrew, nomination of, 101, 102, 103.

Johnston, John D., letter to, 9.

Jones, Thomas D., reminiscences by, 103.

Julian, George W., reminiscences by, 99.

Kalamazoo, speech, 15.

Keckley, Elizabeth, *Behind the Scenes*, 110–11.

Kelley, William D., reminiscences by, 100, 101.

Kentucky, in Civil War, 77; Lincoln family in, 72, 73.

Know Nothing Party, x, 4.

Koerner, Gustave, letter to, 12; *Memoirs*, xv.

Ku Klux Klan, x.

Laird rams, 92.

Lamon, Ward Hill, buys Herndon manuscripts, 28; letters from Herndon, 96; *Life of Abraham Lincoln*, 20–24; *Recollections of Abraham Lincoln*, 23–24; on Lincoln's religion, 117.

Langdon, John, xn.

Lapsley, Arthur Brooks, *Writings of Abraham Lincoln*, 10–11.

Learned, Marion Dexter, *Abraham Lincoln: An American Migration*, 67.

Leech, Margaret, *Reveille in Washington*, 78n.

Lemen, James, letter to, 12.

Lexington, Lincoln in, 76–77; Mary Todd in, 77.

Lincoln, Abraham (grandfather), death, 68.

Lincoln, Abraham, ancestry, 65–69; assassination, 78, 121–25; bibliography, 128–29; biography, advantages of, xiv–xvii; birthplace, 68–69; cabinet appointments, 104; cartoons, 120; childhood, 31, 68–69; chronology, 69–72; commander-in-chief, 89–90; congressional service, 72; election (1860), 83–84; foreign affairs, 92–94; finances, 111–12; forged letters, 12, 14–15; Gettysburg Address, 94–95; health, 113–14; legal career, 79–81; legends, 125–28; legislative service, 72; liquor, 70, 115–16; literary art, 114–15; marriage, 32n; misdated letters, 9–10; nomination (1860), 82–83, 104; parentage, 65–69; personality, 104–08; photographs, 118–20; political career, 81–89; president-elect, 84; Radicals and, 95–96; reconstruction policy, 95–96; religion, 20, 23, 30, 31, 32n, 117–18; reminiscences of, 96–104; secession policy, 84–85.

Lincoln, Mrs. Abraham, health, 113–14; finances, 112; studies of, 108–11. *See also* Todd, Mary.

Lincoln, Mordecai, descendants, 66.

Lincoln, Robert Todd, letter from, 3–4; makes father's papers available, 33–34, 35; opposes publication of *Herndon's Lincoln*, 32.

Lincoln, Samuel, 67, 73.

Lincoln, Thomas, alleged photograph, 119; characterized, 21, 39, 54, 69.

Lincoln, Waldo, *History of the Lincoln Family*, 67.

Lincoln family, history, 65–69.

Lincoln-Douglas Debates, 4, 81–82.

Linder, Usher F., *Reminiscences*, xv.

Locke, David R., reminiscences by, 100.

Lorant, Stefan, *Lincoln, His Life in Photographs*, 119–20.

"Lost Speech," 39, 54.

Louisiana, reconstruction in, 95.

Lowell, James Russell, interpretation of Lincoln, 127.

Lusk, Edward, letter to, 4.

Luthin, Reinhard H., *First Lincoln Campaign*, 83–84.

Luthin, Reinhard H., and Carman, Harry J., *Lincoln and the Patronage*, 87–88.

McCarthy, Charles H., *Lincoln's Plan of Reconstruction*, 95–96.

McClellan, George B., characterization, xvi, 61; relations with Lincoln, 102.

McClure, Alexander K., *Abraham Lincoln and Men of War-Times*, 101–02; on Johnson's nomination, 103.

McClure's Magazine, 38.

McDowell, Irvin, and Radicals, 86.

McLean, John, papers of, 82; political career, 83.

Mason, James, seizure of, 92; sketch, 93.

Maurice, Sir Frederick, *Statesmen and Soldiers of the Civil War*, 89n.

Meade, George G., 89.

Melloni, Macedonio, letter to, 14.

Mencken, H. L., quoted, 52.

Meserve, Frederick Hill, and Sandburg, Carl, *Photographs of Abraham Lincoln*, 118–19.

Monaghan, Jay, *Diplomat in Carpet Slippers*, 92–94; *Lincoln Bibliography*, ixn, 10, 128–29.

Morean, A. B., letter to, 9.

Morgan, John Hunt, sketch, 77.

Morgan, Richard Price, 98.

Mudd, Samuel A., 125.

Napoleon III, 92, 93.

New Jersey, Lincoln family in, 73.

New Salem, Lincoln in, 73–75.

Newton, Joseph Fort, *Lincoln and Herndon*, 105–06.

Nicolay, Helen, *Personal Traits of Abraham Lincoln*, 106–08.

Nicolay, John G., controversy with McClure, 102; memoranda of, 106–07; *Short Life of Abraham Lincoln*, 41.

Nicolay, John G., and Hay, John, *Abraham Lincoln: A History*, 33–37; *Complete Works* (1894), 3–6; *Complete Works* (1905), 6–11.

Norton, Charles Eliot, interpretation of Lincoln, 127.

Oakleaf, Joseph Benjamin, Lincoln Bibliography, 129.

Owens, Mary, Lincoln's courtship, 23, 34.

Palmer, John M., *Washington, Lincoln, Wilson: Three War Statesmen*, 89n.

Palmerston, Henry John Temple, Lord, 93.

Paris (Ill.), speech, 10.

Parker, Theodore, correspondence with Herndon, 105–06.

Parks, Samuel C., and Howells biography, 18.

Patronage, Lincoln's use of, 87–88.

Pennsylvania, Lincoln family in, 73.

Peoria, speech, 15.

Peoria "truce," 54, 70.

Petersen, William F., *Lincoln-Douglas: The Weather as Destiny*, 113–14.

Phillips, Isaac N., *Abraham Lincoln, By Some Men Who Knew Him*, 98–99.

Phillips, Wendell, 127.

Piatt, Donn, reminiscences by, 99.

Pickett, George E., letter to, 8, 116.

Poore, Ben Perley, reminiscences by, 99.

Pope, John, and Radicals, 86.

Potter, David M., *Lincoln and His Party in the Secession Crisis*, 84–85.

Pratt, Harry E., *Lincoln, 1809–1839*, 69–72; *Lincoln, 1840–1846*, 69–72; *Personal Finances of Abraham Lincoln*, 111–12.

Proclamation of Emancipation, painting, 100.

Quaife, Milo M., review of *Prairie Years*, 52n.

Randall, James G., *Civil War and Reconstruction*, 49; *Constitutional Problems under Lincoln*, 90–92; Foreword by, 129; *Lincoln the President*, 58–62.

Radical Republicans, plan of reconstruction, 95–96; and Lincoln's assassination, 124.

"Rebecca" letters, 54.

Reconstruction, Lincoln and, 95–96.

Reed, James A., on Lincoln's religion, 117.

Reep, Thomas P., *Lincoln at New Salem*, 74.

Reeves, Owen T., reminiscences by, 98.

Republican Party, attitude towards secession, 84–85; convention, 1860, 101; growth of, in Illinois, 106; and patronage, 88; Radical members, 86.

Rice, Allen Thorndike, *Reminiscences of Abraham Lincoln*, 99–100.

Richards, John T., *Lincoln the Lawyer-Statesman*, 79.

Rickard, Sarah, 110.

Robinson, Luther E., *Abraham Lincoln As a Man of Letters*, 115.

Rocca, Raymond G., "Fascist Propaganda and a Lincoln Forgery," 14n.

Russell, Lord John, 93.

Rutledge, Ann, death of, effect on Lincoln, 113; Herndon's lecture, 28; romance with Lincoln, 23, 30, 34.

Rutledge, R. B., letters to Herndon, 96.

Ste. Marie Brass Band and Ste. Cecilia Society, 15.

Sandburg, Carl, *Prairie Years*, 49–52; *War Years*, 56–58.

Sandburg, Carl, and Angle, Paul M., *Mary Lincoln, Wife and Widow*, 110.

Sandburg, Carl, and Meserve, Frederick Hill, *Photographs of Abraham Lincoln*, 118–19.

Sangamon County Fair Grounds, xii.

Scott, Winfield, reports to Lincoln, 36.

Scott Club Speech, 13.

Secession, Lincoln's policy, 84–85.

Second Inaugural Address, 115.

Seward, William H., attitude towards secession, 84–85; political career, 83; sketch, 93.

Shaw, Albert, *Abraham Lincoln: A Cartoon History*, 120.

Shields, James, 34.

Sherman, William T., relations with Lincoln, 102.

Sickles, Daniel E., on Lincoln's religion, 117.

Slavery, Confederate plans to abolish, 93; Lincoln's experience with, 77.

Slidell, John, seizure of, 92; sketch, 93.

Sparks, Edwin Erle, *Lincoln-Douglas Debates*, 81–82.

Speed, Joshua F., Lincoln visits, 70.

Springfield, speech, 10; Lincoln in, 73, 75–76.

Stanton, Edwin M., characterized, xvi, 61, 121–22; and Lincoln's assassination, 123–24; Lincoln's relations with, 102; and Radicals, 86.

Starr, John W., Jr., Lincoln bibliography, 129.

Stephens, Alexander H., letter to, 12.

Stephenson, Nathaniel W., *Lincoln*, 44–46, 59n.

Stern, Philip Van Doren, *Life and Writings*, 15–16.

Stevens, Thaddeus, Lincoln's relations with, 102; and Radicals, 86.

Stowe, Harriet Beecher, sketch, 52.

Sumner, Charles, sketch, 93.

Surratt, John H., and assassination of Lincoln, 121; capture, 122.

Surratt, Mrs. Mary E., and assassination of Lincoln, 125; clemency, 121, 122; executed, 126.

Swett, Leonard, letter on Lincoln's nomination, 104; letters to Herndon, 96; reminiscences by, 99, 105; and Weik's *Real Lincoln*, 104.

Sympson, Alexander, letter to, 10.

Taft, Dr. Charles S., reminiscences by, 103.

Tandy, Francis D., edits Lincoln's works, 7.

Taney, Roger, controversy with Lincoln, 79.

Tarbell, Ida M., *Early Life of Abraham Lincoln*, 38; *In the Footsteps of the Lincolns*, 72–73; *Life of Abraham Lincoln*, 38–40.

Taylor, E. D., letter to, 15.

Taylor, Zachary, eulogy, 13.

Teillard, Dorothy Lamon, edits Lamon's *Recollections*, 24.

Temperance, and Lincoln, 115–16.

Tennessee, reconstruction in, 95.

Thomas, Benjamin P., *Lincoln: 1847–1853*, 69–72; *Lincoln's New Salem*, 73–74.

Todd, Mary, health, 113–14; Lexington girlhood, 77; Lincoln's courtship, 23; marriage, 30. *See also* Lincoln, Mrs. Abraham.

Todd, Robert S., home of, 77.

Townsend, William H., *Abraham Lincoln Defendant*, 47, 48n; *Lincoln and His Wife's Home Town*, 76–77; *Lincoln and Liquor*, 115–16; *Lincoln the Litigant*, 47, 48n.

Tracy, Gilbert A., *Uncollected Letters*, 11–12.

Tree, Lambert, reminiscences by, 103.

Trumbull, Lyman, 82.

Urbana, speech, 15.

Virginia, Lincoln family in, 73; reconstruction in, 95.

Wade, Benjamin F., political career, 83; and Radicals, 86.

Warren, Louis A., illegitimacy of Nancy Hanks, 32n; *Lincoln's Parentage and Childhood*, 68–69.

Washburne, Elihu B., papers of, 82; reminiscences by, 99.

Washington, D.C., during Civil War, 78–79, 89.

Weed, Thurlow, characterized, 93; influence sought, 87.

Weik, Jesse W., letters from Herndon, 96; *Real Lincoln*, 104–05.

Weik, Jesse W., and Herndon, William H., *Herndon's Lincoln*, 28–33.

Weldon, Lawrence, reminiscences by, 99.

Welles, Gideon, 104.

Wessen, Ernest J., "Campaign Lives of Abraham Lincoln, 1860," 17n.

West Virginia, 95.

White, Horace, edits *Herndon's Lincoln*, 33; letters to Herndon, 96.

Whitman, Walt, interpretation of Lincoln, 127; reminiscences by, 99; sketch, 52.

Whitney, Henry C., *Life on the Circuit*, 80–81; Lincoln speech, 80; "Lost Speech," 39, 54; reminiscences by, 97, 105.

Williams, T. Harry, *Lincoln and the Radicals*, 86–87.

Wilson, Woodrow, 92.

Wilson, Rufus Rockwell, *Intimate Memories of Lincoln*, 103–04; *Lincoln Among His Friends*, 102–03.

Woldman, Albert A., *Lawyer Lincoln*, 79–80.

Young Men's Lyceum speech, 9.

Zane, Charles S., reminiscences by, 103.